UNIQUE

UNIQUE
KELLY HOLMES
A MEMOIR

MIRROR BOOKS

To all those who have felt different,
have not had your voices heard,
don't feel that you are living your best life,
feel undervalued or scared,
I hear you.

Just remember the other side of pain is beauty,
because it is unique and purposeful for each and
every one of us, it can teach us things that we
would not be able to see otherwise.

To Dad,

Without you my life would have
never been the same.
I love you x

To Mother Dear,

I hope you can see me now,
keep sending the butterflies.

MIRROR BOOKS

Kelly Holmes collaborated with Gemma Aldridge.

1

First published in hardback in Great Britain and Ireland in 2023 by Mirror Books, a Reach PLC business.

www.mirrorbooks.co.uk
@TheMirrorBooks

ISBN: 9781915306760
Hardback ISBN: 9781915306463
eBook ISBN: 9781915306470

Photographic acknowledgements:
Kelly Holmes personal collection, Alamy, Reach Plc.

Every effort has been made to trace copyright.
Any oversights will be rectified in future editions.

Production: Christine Costello

Printed and bound by CPI Group (UK) Ltd,
Croydon, CR0 4YY.

MIX
Paper | Supporting
responsible forestry
FSC® C171272

CONTENTS

Five Years

FIVE YEARS. WE HEAR ABOUT THAT TIME PERIOD ALL through our lives, don't we? *Where do you see yourself in five years' time? What's your five-year plan?* At school, in job interviews, even among friends and at family gatherings, people always want to know what's coming next. It's easy to answer those questions when you have a dream or a clear and achievable goal in your head, as I've found out over the years.

I knew when I was 14 without doubt that I wanted to be a soldier in the British Army and five years later I was serving the Crown and my country. I also knew I wanted to be an Olympic champion and it was five years after joining the British Army that I started competing internationally in pursuit of Olympic glory. Five years after that I was leaving the army to concentrate full-time on my career as an elite athlete.

It might have taken me another few years to become the first British woman to win two individual gold medals at the same Olympic Games but in my heart I always knew I would do it. All through my life, I've had goals and aspirations and every time,

I've fought to make them happen because I never give up, it's in my DNA.

But what happens when the thing you think could make you happiest in the world seems out of your grasp? How do you even start to fight for something that seems so far out of reach? What happens when any plans you make get turned upside down after a life event totally floors you? Five years ago, despite all my achievements in life, that was the situation I was in…

In 2017, my mum Pam, or 'Mother Dear' as I called her, died aged 65 from a rare form of blood cancer called Myeloma. Her death completely destroyed me, it turned my world upside down and I felt like a part of my heart died with her – it still feels that way sometimes today. But when she died I realised something about myself that changed everything else in my life forever.

I realised how much I was hiding away from the world and not really living; how I could never truly be happy until I was honest about who I am – a gay woman who has led a life of fear, standing behind my achievements so I would never have to face judgement or persecution for just being me and loving the people I want to love. I knew inside I had to change something otherwise one day it would be the end of my life and I never would have been truly free or truly me. So that was where my journey began. In many ways it was the toughest journey of my life – and there have been a few!

It was five hard years after that dreadful realisation that I came out publicly for the first time at the age of 52 (or 39+13 as I like to call it!). You might wonder why, in the 21st century, I've felt unable to be honest about my sexuality when society has moved on so much and being gay is so much more accepted now than it once was. That is why I'm writing this book.

The truth is that my experiences as a young woman scarred me to a point where I've been paralysed with fear of punishment for my sexuality for most of my adult life. You see, when I fulfilled my first big dream of enrolling in the army and pledging my allegiance to the Crown, I also unknowingly joined an institution that outlawed homosexuality and would make me a criminal just because I was attracted to women instead of men.

Not many people seem to know, but even though it was decriminalised for civilians in 1967, the ban on being gay in the military remained in force right up until the European Court of Human Rights ruled it illegal in 2000, long after I'd served my nine and a half years in the army.

Throughout my athletics career, being made a Dame, an Honorary Colonel and a household name as Team GB's 'Golden Girl', it might have seemed to the public like I had the world at my feet, but deep down I was terrified, just waiting for someone to 'out' me as being gay. Like so many others, I learnt early on to hide my feelings away to protect myself and I never got over that trauma. I was convinced if I was found out I would be publicly shamed, stripped of my military honours and even prosecuted for breaking the law when I was a serving soldier.

So I spent 34 years trapped in a cage of my own fear, speaking quietly, dressing conservatively, living my life in black and white instead of the bright colours I like wearing now. I said 'no' to things I would have loved to do, avoided new friendships and turned down work opportunities, just so I didn't draw attention to myself or have to have conversations about my personal life. I never let anyone get too close in case I had to lie to them about who I really was and avoided any personal subjects in media interviews.

I lived two separate lives in public and in private and by the time Mother Dear got her cancer diagnosis in 2014, it was tearing me apart. Despite all my achievements the one thing she wished for me was that one day I would just set myself free by being open about my sexuality, so I could live my life for me. It wasn't easy and it was a slow process but just short of five years after I lost her, I finally did it.

Those five years transformed my life beyond recognition. It's been a journey of grief, anxiety, stress, mental breakdown, burnout, healing, self-discovery and finally a celebration of who I am. I've gone from hiding away in the shadows to living my life in full rainbow colour and now I say 'yes' to things instead of 'no'. I've gone from living in the shade of other high achievers, to standing in the spotlight, and although it still doesn't always come naturally, I'm happier than I've ever been. I've even fallen in love with a wonderful woman who I now share my new life with, but more on that later…

When I've told my story before, I've always hidden the real Kelly, and left out a huge part of me that makes me who I am. Now it's time to celebrate it. This is the true story of Dame Kelly Holmes, who I am, and how I got here. I think Mother Dear would be proud.

1

Black, White, Gold and Rainbows

STANDING ON STAGE LOOKING OUT AT THE SEA OF rainbow flags and glitter-covered faces, my heart started pounding in my chest. As I stood there, wearing my own rainbow outfit – a long, multicoloured caftan with a Progress flag full length on the back, like the one Jason Donovan wore in *Joseph and The Amazing Technicolor Dreamcoat* – the roar of the crowd around me echoed, and the enormity of the occasion dawned on me. It was London Pride in 2022 and there I was; centre stage.

My mind whirred. What the hell did I think I was doing?! It was massive enough coming out in a national newspaper and making my documentary which had taken months to curate and edit so that I could tell my story as I wanted. It was another thing entirely appearing on stage in front of hundreds of thousands of people in Trafalgar Square in London city centre. Being there with what felt like the entire LGBTQIA community (a title I had now become accustomed to) and allies of our capital city staring at me, I started to wonder if I'd bitten off more than I could chew. I have no idea what they were expecting of me. If anything, I wasn't sure if I should say something profound or insightful about equality and diversity or make a big political statement, but all I did know is that I wanted to say something from my heart.

Back stage I'd scribbled on a notepaper in a tent. None other than the tent Emeli Sandé was getting ready in before her performance. The last time I saw her was at the launch party of her album. I was still a bit starstruck, after all I had been a fan for years!

I had spent decades avoiding Pride and all things related with it for my entire adult life because I was convinced if I was seen to be celebrating the gay community, then straight away they would make assumptions about me too. That was my biggest fear of all. Look; I had no doubt, of course, that a few people along the way knew for sure, and also that a huge amount of people who followed my career had assumed I was gay, but in my mind assumption was not MY freedom.

Now, whatever anyone thought – that I had lived a lie, that I was ashamed or hiding a secret – was not my concern. They were not living my life! Finally it was time for me to tell my story, in my own words and give myself the freedom to speak.

As a soldier in the British Army, I've been on parade more times than I can remember. In my career as a world-class and Olympic athlete, I've had my share of time on podiums, along with some incredible homecoming parades. Trafalgar Square had an energy I'd not witnessed since the announcement of the Olympic Games in 2005, and the atmosphere was like nothing I've ever experienced.

BLACK, WHITE, GOLD AND RAINBOWS

The crowd was deafening; singing, cheering, laughing. Faces smiling and carefree. People were standing on the statue plinths, hanging over railings, messing about in the water fountain and waving their different community flags loud and proud. The parade was still going, music echoed in the distance, this was such a massive event to be part of. Being introduced to the crowd just after they had announced an estimated one and a half million people were in attendance, filled me with a euphoria, my heart was racing, butterflies in my stomach. I got this overwhelming sense of emotion running through my body, because this was the start of a new life for me.

My name was in lights and I had the platform to say whatever I wanted. The organisers had told me I had a few minutes before I would introduce Emeli on stage so I was a nervous wreck even before I looked out at the enormous crowd.

Having been a professional speaker for many years, travelling around the world for corporate engagements and motivational speeches, these days I rarely use notes, I don't really get nervous, I just feel an adrenaline rush. But today I was a bag of nerves, I just wanted the words to be right. I pulled the folded piece of paper from the pocket of my jean shorts, took a deep breath and started to speak into the microphone…

"For those who don't know me, I am an Honorary Colonel with the Royal Armoured Corps Training Regiment, I am a Dame Commander of The British Empire, I am the first British woman in the history of the Olympic Games to win two gold medals at the same games, I am mixed-race and I am also a gay woman…"

The crowd erupted and I had a lump in my throat as I carried on, tears pricking my eyes. My voice got stronger with every word.

"For 34 years I have never been able to say those words until two weeks ago, due to the fear of judgement and retribution that was instilled in me since the age of 18, because the laws in the military and being in the public eye didn't allow me to do it. I could never speak before but I have realised no matter if you are lesbian, gay, bisexual, transgender, queer, intersex, asexual, black, white, short, tall, big, small, however you identify and even straight (as I giggled), we have the right to stand side by side with each other, we all deserve to have our voices heard.

"All I can definitely say now is I'm 52, I'm never going to live behind that curtain again. Freedom is my voice!"

The crowd roared and I felt myself embody a campaigner, asking the crowd to chant with me, "FREEDOM IS MY VOICE, FREEDOM IS MY VOICE, FREEDOM IS MY VOICE!". I felt like I was in a different world: invincible, important, influential but most of all accepted. Proud doesn't even get close to the feeling I experienced that moment.

* * * * *

As with many life-changing moments, the Pride stage nearly didn't happen. I still laugh at the thought of it. When Gok Wan messaged me to join him and the ITV team on their double-decker bus in the Pride parade the weekend after my documentary aired, I was excited at the thought of finally joining in on all the fun that I had missed for so many years. This was my first Pride EVER! But, equally, I was nervous.

It turned out my first one was in a good year. The UK's Pride march started in 1972, inspired by the Stonewall riots in New York which sent a shockwave through the gay community and triggered gay pride movements around the world. 2022 marked 50 years of celebrations and protest, and London was set to be bigger than ever before.

There were more than 600 groups and 30,000 people registered to take part in the parade, the public lined the route as floats, bands, dance troupes and lobbying groups led the procession through the city from Hyde Park Corner to Trafalgar Square. Talk about a baptism of fire.

"It'll be fine, stick with me and we're on the ITV bus," Gok reassured me when I told him how nervous I was. "Everyone will be there together."

So after a couple of drinks for Dutch courage at the ITV rooftop party, we all meandered down to the bus. Gok, Lorraine Kelly, Philip Schofield, Alison Hammond, Linda Robson, my relatively new partner Lou and I all piled onto the bus, ready to party. It was Phil's first Pride too, since he came out at the age of 60 back in February 2020, so I felt a bit of solidarity with him. We climbed the stairs to the top deck, chatting, taking selfies, dancing to Gok DJing and going live on Instagram. I realised, when the bus before us started moving and we weren't actually following, that something was wrong.

"The buses in front are going," I said, starting to wonder if we were in the right place. But just as I was saying it a bloke appeared in front of us with what looked like an oily engine part in his equally oil-stained hand. "I'm sorry guys, we've broken down," he said. "We'll be here for a while."

Suddenly panic set in. The bus was surrounded with people from this huge parade, the different communities and organisations in all their glory. Music was playing from the other buses and the bands below. There were dancers and people singing. Banners and flags flying everywhere.

"Let's get out and walk," suggested one of the ITV crew. I just looked at Phil and Gok and gulped! Alison thought it was too far, especially in the sweltering heat.

"We'll give it a while, see if they fix it," someone else suggested. But after 20 minutes it became clear we wouldn't be going anywhere on the bus.

So we began walking together. It was one of the most empowering things I've ever done in my life, as people along the way were congratulating me. It was such a positive atmosphere and for the first time I felt that my uniqueness was what made me belong, not what made me different.

Time was ticking and I wasn't going to make it to the end of the route and to the back of the huge stage on Trafalgar Square in time for my speech. So drag legend Courtney Act said she would walk with me, cutting through the streets of London. All I could think was that, out of everyone there and me trying to be slightly incognito away from the parade, I was with Courtney, all glammed up and looking spectacular in a rainbow gown, and the most fabulous coloured wig. Towering over me in her six-inch heels, we giggled with one another as she illuminated our way through the backstreets to the stage entrance.

Incredibly, in a blink of an eye, a fortnight into my journey, standing on a stage with no curtain, I had my first initiation of Pride. To make it more awesome and overwhelming at the same time Emeli, who I'd been listening to in my living room two weeks earlier, was waiting in the wings to come on stage after I announced her. Not long after, I was back on stage standing next to her with some other people I later came to know very well, singing MY song live. Yes, MY song – *Read All About It*.

I will admit I had a few tears that day, it felt like my life was being transformed. I was so emotional about what was happening that it was hard to digest the enormity of it all. What a crazy experience.

I'd made my vow in front of the world to never live behind

a curtain again and was now accountable as the thousands of voices chanted my words "freedom is my voice" back at me and I felt the weight of 34 years finally lifting from my shoulders.

The rest of the day passed in a blur with music, hype and introductions. After meeting Emeli and her partner, Jenny (Emeli's friend and PA at the time) introduced me to DIVA publisher Linda Riley – 'Head Lesbian' as I get told, trans couple and activists, Hannah and Jake Graf, as well as, Dawn Butler MP, an amazing LGBTQIA ally. Some of us went out for dinner at The Ivy with amazing, charming, strong, brilliant power women. I was just so overwhelmed. Lou and I then got rather drunk as we danced the night away at Gok's place where he was DJing again.

When I look back, 'surreal' doesn't even begin to cover it. But it was real, and here I am.

2

—

Unique

I'VE MET A LOT OF PEOPLE WHO SAY THEY KNEW even when they were kids at school that they were gay, as if they were born waving a rainbow flag or something. That was never how it was for me. For most of my early life it never even crossed my mind that I might grow up to fancy women instead of men or that this fact would affect how I lived my life for so many years. Perhaps that was because back then sexuality wasn't really spoken about as much, or maybe because there was so much going on in my life when I was a child, it was the last thing on my mind. In any case, most of my formative years were lived in a time before I had any inkling that I liked girls instead of boys.

I guess if you ask me how I felt when I was a kid, the only word to describe it is 'unique' and I still wear that title with pride now. Why would I want to be just like everyone else?

From the moment in April 1970 when I was born at Pembury hospital in Kent, I suppose I was that little bit different. I was the mixed-race baby of a white teenage mum, who'd fallen pregnant by accident after a fling with a Jamaican man her parents strongly disapproved of. Mum was 17 and hadn't long been out of school herself when she found herself with a child of her own to look after.

Looking back now, she was really only a kid herself when I came along, so it must have been terrifying for her. In the almost-entirely white, tiny, blink-and-you-miss-it village of Hildenborough in Kent, where Mum was raised in a traditional working-class suburban family, I was certainly unique. Lots of people probably used less kind words about me too and there's no question that made things hard for both Mum and me those first few years.

Mum's parents, housewife Elsie and farrier Percy Norman, had been horrified when she told them she was expecting a baby at such a young age and even more horrified that the baby was going to be 'black'. Mixed-race relationships were still frowned upon by people of my grandparents' generation back then and especially in the super-conservative community where they lived. They didn't approve of Mum's Jamaican boyfriend, so they rejected me when I came along even though I was their flesh and blood. I guess that was my first experience of being discriminated against, luckily I wasn't old enough to know.

Before I was born, my nan and grandad told Mum she'd have to "find a way to look after herself before she could look after me." So basically she could get rid of me or leave home and try her chances finding somewhere else to live. She was all alone in the world except for the man who got her pregnant; a man she told me later had no interest in being any kind of father to me. I still like to think that she must have loved me so much that she was willing to give up her family and her home and start a new life with someone like that just so she could keep me. But it wasn't as easy as that back then.

Over the next few months she moved into a mother and baby unit in Lee, in the London borough of Lewisham. She tried to make a go of her relationship but the cracks soon started to show. I don't know what happened or the details of how Derrick Holmes and his family treated Mum and me. Mum always found it hard to talk about those early days. Recently my brother Danny (who you will meet later) told me that May – who would have been my nan – did look after me a few times during my first couple of months when Mum went to work. But after the relationship with Derrick broke down, Mum found herself alone with a tiny baby.

Society in the 1970s wasn't a friendly place for single mothers, especially those who had a mixed-race baby before they were married. There was no support available and with no other option she returned to her family out of desperation, but that meant she had to give me up and put me into care. I hate to think of how hard it must have been for her when she was still so young. I think about the young people I work with now through my charity the Dame Kelly Holmes Trust and I see kids the same age as Mum was when she had me and it makes me sad for her and proud of how hard she tried.

Maybe it's no shock that in that world I ended up at St George's children's home on the outskirts of Tunbridge Wells when I was only six months old. Ironically, in a way, that home was the only place I actually did fit in because sadly it was full of little mixed-race and black children who had either been rejected by their families or by society because of the colour of their skin – or were with a parent like my mum. I don't know the exact details of how I ended up there because even in her later years, Mum didn't like to revisit the distant past. There are still huge gaps in my understanding of the first few years of my life, which is something I really struggle with to this day. I'm not surprised Mum didn't like talking about it given how hard she'd tried to keep me and how traumatic it must have been for her to leave me in that big Victorian house full of children and babies, for someone else to look after.

The reason I'm telling you this is that one thing I've learnt when reflecting on my life is that the trauma you go through as a child can stay with you for years and haunt you if you don't address it. One of my earliest memories is of standing up in a cot as I clung onto the wooden bars and looked out over the large room in the children's home. There's a photograph of me there, which I saw years later. The room was filled with other children and it was only in recent years I realised (when looking at photos that I had been sent by a lady who had apparently been one of my carers) that almost every other child in there was black or mixed-race.

It never occurred to me as a child that there was a connection between skin colour and the children who found themselves in a home for abandoned kids – or that my race was to do with why I was rejected by my own family. Now, sadly I realise all too well the reasons why. It took me decades to accept that racism played such a big part in my life story and especially the way I started out.

When people asked me whether I'd ever experienced racism I used to just say no without thinking, because no one had ever abused me in the street or called me racial slurs to my face. It's only now that I realise looking back at my life the insidious impact it had on me and still has on so many people around the world today.

When the murder of George Floyd by police in the US sparked the Black Lives Matter movement around the world in 2020 and people started asking me about my experiences as a mixed-race woman, I started to properly address how it has affected me. I also thought how life would have been so different if it had been influenced by the cultures of both sides of my birth parents.

Talking about our early life together often caused conflict between me and Mum, right up until about 10 years ago when I went on Piers Morgan's *Life Stories*. That hit her especially hard and we had a massive fall-out over me doing the show, but I felt I had a right to.

The ironic thing is that I fought so hard to tell the story of where I came from, yet I was still hiding my sexuality. How I kept that away from Piers Morgan was a miracle! In hindsight I can see how that must have seemed confusing to my mum and I wish we hadn't wasted precious time fighting about it. One thing about losing someone is that it's so bloody finite. There are still so many things I want to ask her and, while writing this book, I've wished she was here a thousand times so I could ask her to fill in the gaps.

I told my life story before in my autobiography *Black, White and Gold* in 2005, but I always knew there were big pieces of the puzzle missing but I was too scared to go digging up the past. This time, I wanted to find out as much as I possibly could and share it with you. Reflecting on over 50 years, especially with peri-menopausal 'brain fog' has been interesting to say the least!

* * * * *

What I do know is that Mum tried her best for me from the start and she even left a promising career in London as a diamond grader and cutter for De Beers Diamond Trading Company when I was three years old, and got herself a job at Unigate Dairies in the laboratory testing milk samples because it was close to St George's, so she could come and see me as often as she liked.

But it was so distressing every time she had to go home without me. I would ball my eyes out and so would she as it was so heart-wrenching for her, when she had to leave me in my bed with my cuddly toys. All I wanted was to be cuddled by her. Every time she left, I was terrified she wasn't going to come back for me and that I would never see her again.

The impact that's had on me in adulthood is huge, I'm sure. I have had abandonment issues and for years I still needed to have something weighted on my feet to comfort me when I was trying to sleep, a triggering reminder of what I used to have for comfort at the end of my bed in the home. It sounds crazy but I bought one of those weighted blankets a few years ago and it really helped.

There have been impacts on how I deal with the people around me too. I'm such a 'people pleaser', terrified of upsetting anyone or disappointing them. In relationships I struggle to let my guard down – all because the sense of rejection and aban-donment I felt as a child still lives on inside me. I was always terrified of being left, which either made me push people away or not want too much attachment, so as not to get hurt.

It must have been psychologically scarring for Mum too, I can't imagine what that must have been like for a teenager, to be torn between her own parents and the child she loved so much. I believe Mum wanted for me to have a better life than she could offer me until she got back on her feet and that's why she put me in care. I don't think she ever intended for me to be there long term and she certainly never imagined the damage that my fear of abandonment would cause me in my later life as a result – but there's no doubt damage was done.

For years after I left St George's, I had nightmares about Mum taking me somewhere and leaving me, and me searching endlessly to find her again. And it definitely made it more difficult for me to be open about my sexuality in later life, too, because I've always been scared people would reject me for that as well. I have no doubt those early experiences shaped and affected me as an adult.

In October 2019, when I led a group of runners for the second year running, on a charity expedition 'Sport with a Purpose' to Malawi, we visited an orphanage called Open Arms, which 'believes that every child has the right to survival and development'.

Prior to going in, we were told about the children that were currently there and when I walked in I became so overwhelmed with emotions I just broke down crying and had to leave. Walking into that room, I suddenly had a bout of anxiety and flashbacks to the cot, the bed (in the home) and the pangs of pain and endless crying when my mum had to leave me there.

Years later, after my Olympic wins, I found out it could have been much worse than being in and out of a children's home. Mum kept it a secret for decades but the pressure from my grandparents to give me up had become so great that at one point she'd even agreed for the carers at St George's to find a couple to permanently adopt me.

Social services came to the home to take me away but when the other woman took me in her arms, Mum broke down and couldn't go through with it. She loved me too much. This apparently happened three times as they tried to force her to sign the papers, but she wouldn't! When she told me that story, I saw the pain she felt and how she was reliving it as she spoke. I understood then for the first time how hard it was for her to talk about. Maybe it's true that sometimes you have to hit rock bottom for things to get better. Eventually Mum got me back and that was what mattered as she ended up being the most important person in my life.

I reckon it set the precedent for the rest of my life. You don't get many mixed-race, female, gay sergeants in the army who go on to win double Olympic gold and then have a career in TV. It might have made the start of my life difficult but I feel grateful to be who I am because it's brought some wonderful experiences and amazing people into my life too.

I've carried the word 'unique' with me all through my journey as an antidote to the idea of being the odd one out, weird or different. It's meant many things to me over the years and given me strength in many situations, and allowed me to own my differences at times when I've felt alone, judged or misunderstood and that's why it's the title of this book.

3

Brown Girl In
The Ring

I'VE ALWAYS HAD A REALLY STRONG VIEW THAT
what makes someone a parent has nothing to do with DNA
and everything to do with love, care and attention. I'm a great
believer that the step mums and dads, grandparents, foster
parents, carers, social workers and respite carers of this world
who give love and support to children who aren't related to
them by blood are the real heroes of our society. They love and
care for children out of choice; not obligation and somehow
that makes it all the more special.

Having children was something I had never really wanted
myself, because I was more intent on focusing on my career, and
it turned out my lifestyle has never really been right for moth-
erhood anyway. By the way, it is ok to not want children as a
woman and that stigma needs to stop too, something I recently
spoke about on Loose Women. But I did consider fostering or

adopting when I was in my 30s, because I think the role those people do is just so important.

The man who inspired my views on parents by putting an end to the turbulent beginning of my life and teaching me what it is to be a great one was my dad. No, not Derrick, who had, by then, disappeared without trace but Mick Norris; the man who has become more of a father to me than words can describe. An old school friend of Mum's, who was reunited with her when I was about four, he is calm, laid back, quiet and unassuming and utterly reliable. When they started dating, he fell madly in love with my mum, and by extension he loved me too, from day one, without question, as his own. I think that's pretty amazing, especially given that it was going to be very obvious he wasn't my biological father, something that didn't even occur to me until years later.

Dad, as I have called him for almost five decades, was a painter and decorator who worked with his father, Geoff, and was super close to his family. While mum's parents were slowly coming to terms at the idea of me in their world, Mick's family welcomed me with open arms from the beginning and Nan Audrey, Grandad Norris and Aunty Sheila quickly became a big part of my childhood.

After a couple of years living in the estate at a smaller house we were moved next to them, into a three-bed red-brick semi-detached council house, complete with a coal bunker in the garden and metal windows, where I regularly had to scrape the ice of from the inside of my bedroom as it was so cold! I loved the close family stability of living next to them.

I can't remember exactly when I started calling Mick 'Dad', but I can't imagine anything else now and no one deserves the title more. We didn't have much when I was a kid and money was tight but I didn't feel I went without anything and from school uniforms to holidays at various Butlin's and food on the table, Dad made sure mum and I had what we needed and that I felt loved and wanted and that was what mattered. I feel lucky that he has always been part of my life.

One of my earliest and happiest memories of him, when he was dating my mum, was when he came back from Spain with his mates after a holiday, wearing flowery shirts and singing *Viva Espana* which always made me laugh! He also loves Country & Western films; Clint Eastwood and John Wayne. So much so that, on his 60th birthday, I planned a surprise Country and Western fancy dress party, complete with a Wild West town set called 'Micksville', with bar, jail, hay bales, 'WANTED' signs, a live band and line-dancing instructor.

I bought Dad a complete sheriff's outfit and, as another surprise, I had organised for a horse to be brought down from the local stables to take him to the party, because I wanted him to arrive in style. The animal was huge and I was nearly wetting myself at the thought of how we would hoick him up onto the saddle. If you know my dad, you'll know how hard a task this was, given his personal record for Buckaroo is 0.5 seconds – but I eventually got him down to the party and the smile on his face said it all.

I guess what I'm trying to say is, he's always been there for me and still is. He's been a constant in my life, and he's around at my house every day; feeding The Boys – my five alpacas – or picking me up from the station. Being a good parent is sharing in a child's triumphs, being there to pick them up when they fall and loving every part of them, just as they are, without trying to make them change, and that is what he has done for me.

When I told him I was writing this book and asked him to

know more about my early childhood, he told me something I wish I'd known sooner. Apparently, not long after my parents met, he asked Mum if he could adopt me so I would be his own in law but she said no. I would love to know her reasons but I can't ask her now. I wonder whether she was so traumatised by her experience of social services trying to have me adopted, that she thought giving someone else legal rights over me would mean she risked losing me again if things didn't work out with Mick. I guess now I'll never know but it does feel good to know how desperate Dad was for me to be his, right from the start. He is a man of very little words, and these days I feel like his mother, especially when I keep nagging him to get his hair cut, or wash his car and I get him to bring his washing around because his clothes are always stinking of the bonfire he has each week in my garden (plus I LOVE ironing!).

I never felt a massive maternal calling and I can't say I regret not being a mother because I don't believe in regrets, I believe in making the very best of the life you have, and I'm blessed to have so many wonderful kids in mine. I have ten nieces and nephews (Honey, Archie, Lola, Rosa, Olivia, Lily, Martha, Finley, Poppy and Ada Mae) between my brothers, Kevin, Stuart and Danny, and my sisters Lisa and Penny. They're not allowed to call me the 'A-word' because it makes me feel old, but I love them all to bits and I hope I can be a positive influence in their lives. My dad doesn't read much, like me, but I'm going to make him read this, as I know it will embarrass him. Dad, I love you to bits!

* * * * *

It took me a really long time to realise and accept that even though I *didn't* feel different when I was really young, from the people around me when I was growing up, I reflect on how I may have been treated differently and probably still am now. As a mixed-race kid in 'whiter than white Kent' and in an all-white household, you might wonder how I didn't feel the odd one out from the beginning. I think it's because kids do not know the difference in others unless it's pointed out to them and I just did all the same things as my friends and then my siblings Kevin and Stuart – ate the same, enjoyed the same games (when playing out in the streets on my stilts, pogo sticks and Space Hopper was still a thing!) and had the same annoying arguments with my parents. So why would I feel different?

Shortly before my seventh birthday Mum and Mick made it official, getting hitched in the local village church. As their only child, I was of course a bridesmaid, complete with frilly 1970s dress, a bonnet and shiny new shoes. I loved playing up in front of all the guests and posing cheekily for the camera as the wedding pics were taken. It didn't occur to me that it was strange for my mum and dad to be getting married with me there, unlike my friends' parents who had been married before they were born. I don't know if it was because I blocked it out but back then I didn't really have much recollection of life before Mick, so I just accepted our family as it was.

Soon after the wedding, my first brother Kevin was born. That was when everything changed. I remember Mum and Dad bringing him home from the hospital and peeking excitedly at his face wrapped inside the blanket. I threw myself into being a good big sister, playing with him, helping Mum feed, change and bathe him (she must have thought she had her own little live-in maid!). He was my little sidekick and I loved him so much.

Most of the time he wanted to sleep with me and when he was a toddler he kept bringing this tatty blanket into my bed with him but I didn't mind, he was so cute and I was his big sis. I'm not sure if I ever had that one item that stuck to me like his blanket, probably because I was in and out of St George's but I loved having Kevin around, he was my little brother and I became the boss, which suited me fine!

At school, in the playground, my different colour was harder to ignore. "Why are you brown and your brother's white?" the other kids would ask when they met Kevin. Unlike me, Kevin was fair, with white skin and rosy cheeks, he looked nothing like me. I don't think they meant to be nasty, they were just curious.

It was one thing looking different from my classmates but they couldn't understand why I didn't even look like the family they saw collecting me at the school gates. For the first time I remember being conscious of the fact I was different. But the truth was, I didn't really understand either. I wasn't just the only dark-skinned one in my family but in the whole of Hildenborough Primary School.

In 1978 when I was eight years old, the song *Brown Girl In The Ring* by Boney M hit the charts and was played on every radio station every day. The catchy tune and lyrics soon turned it into a playground song. The other kids in my class used to stand around in a big circle with me in the middle as they sang the words: *Brown girl in the ring, tra la la la la...* I loved it. I would dance around and sing... *She looks like a sugar in a plum, plum, plum*! I actually think I liked being the centre of attention, never realising in my naivety that the reason I was always picked to go in the middle was because of my skin colour. I did start to feel uneasy sometimes, just because, by now, I had questions.

On the way back from school one day, I plucked up the courage to ask Mum why I was brown and Kevin was white and that was when she told me that my Dad Mick wasn't in fact my biological father.

"There was another man that I knew before you were born and he's your biological father," she explained. I had no idea what that meant. "He's black and that's why you have darker skin, because you're a mix between him and me."

I knew deep down that Dad loved me but hearing about that other man, I felt hurt and left out and the older I grew, the more difficult it became.

When my youngest brother Stuart came along, I loved him as much as Kev but I was outnumbered – the only girl, the only mixed-race one, the only one with another father that no one ever spoke about because Kevin and Stuart didn't know any different. Plus, the older I got in school the more obvious it became. In school photos they always placed me, the only dark-skinned girl in the middle of the pictures, almost to make a point of it.

It's a strange feeling to grow up a different colour to your family but without any knowledge or experience of your different race or culture. I grew up in a white English family where we ate meat and veg and watched soaps on the telly. The furthest we ever went on holiday was a caravan park on the Isle of Wight and the only foreign food I knew was a Chinese takeaway. Nothing could have felt more distant to me growing up in rural Kent than the island of Jamaica where my biological dad's side of the family was from.

I knew nothing about Jamaican culture and to be honest I have never had any interest in finding out either. It's not that I've ever been ashamed of my colour, it's just that I don't always know how to be or what people expect from a mixed-race British person sometimes because I've been brought up white, if there's such a thing.

When I was researching my documentary *Kelly Holmes: Being*

Me I met wonderful, political activist and LGBTQ+ campaigner Phyll Opoku-Gyimah, known as Lady Phyll. I asked her why she founded UK Black Pride and I remember her saying: "The world doesn't necessarily like black queer women like myself, so when you don't see yourself represented, you create that space and you speak up."

It made me realise how important it is that people can see someone that looks like them, feels like them, sounds like them doing good things and making a difference so they have a role model to look up to. I know everyone has a story. We have no right to 'judge a book by its cover'. I believe people should be heard first and if we just talk more to each other as human beings, there would be far less anguish in the world. I hope now that I'm living authentically, I can be that person for anyone including mixed-race gay women because if I'd seen someone like myself when I was a teenager, my life might have been different.

* * * * *

One thing I've been grateful for all my life is my close group of amazing friends who have been there for me through thick and thin. Most of my closest mates have been in my life since I was just a kid.

If I have one piece of advice to anyone going through a tough personal time, it's to lean on the people who know you best and love you anyway. If I ever felt left out at home when I was a child, when I started secondary school at Hugh Christie's in Tonbridge at the age of 11, I definitely found mine. Not because I was particularly popular or I suddenly fitted in but because I found a group of girls who, just like me, also felt a bit like the odd ones out.

Looking back, maybe all girls at that awkward age feel that way but when I met Kerrie, Lara, and Kim in particular, we felt like it was us against the world. That kind of girl power we had back then (even before the Spice Girls) has seen me through some tough times in my later life. They're the people I text when I'm having a bad day or in need of friend time, they're always there for me.

Kerrie was the first person I met at Hugh Christie's, in the new starters' assembly on my first day. She was fair skinned with frizzy ginger hair and freckles and we hit it off straight away, as I remember thinking she was the only one who had hair almost as crazy as mine.

We went to our first class together and quickly surrounded ourselves with a tight group. There was Duran Duran-mad girly-girl Debbie who towered over the rest of us. I was jealous of her long blonde hair and even longer legs. Kim Ruck was sporty like me and there was Lara, who was the rebel of the group.

The girls were a massive part of my life as a teenager, but during those years my differences and my looks started to bother me loads. Unlike my mum's long brown hair that flowed poker straight down her back, I had an afro that looked like an enormous black ball of cotton wool on top of my head.

One summer, the rest of the girls decided we were all going to grow our hair long over the holidays and come back in September with long, grown-up hairstyles like the women on TV adverts and in magazines.

"What am I going to do? It's not fair," I whined to my mum when I got home from school. "I'm going to be the only one who won't have long hair for the start of the school year."

A few weeks into the school holidays, mum said she would

take me on a train up to Lewisham, Southeast London to get my hair done. Only now do I know why we went to Lewisham. She knew it because it had been where we lived before she took me to the children's home.

"I've found a place where they know how to deal with your kind of hair," she said. "You'll have long hair like the rest of them, I promise."

I was so chuffed as we walked through Lewisham, unknowingly not far from where I spent the first months of my life as a baby. The trend of the time for black women was to apply a perm that let the afro drop into thick loose curls, so that was what I had done. I left that salon walking on air, I was so happy and back home in my bedroom I couldn't stop looking at my new waves in the mirror. But disaster was about to strike.

A couple of weeks later, when I was with Mum, Dad, Kev and Stu down at the beach of Camber Sands in East Sussex, out of nowhere, my hair started to break off in clumps. Horrified, I cried to my mum about what was happening.

"I don't understand," she said, trying not to look panicked and to calm me down as angry tears fell down my face. It turned out mum had no idea how to look after my hair after the perm and that we were meant to go back and get a treatment to stop the ends splitting, putting moisture back into the hair – it was so dry it just broke off.

Weeks later back at school, while my friends were all sporting new long hair, humiliatingly, mine was no longer than an inch all over. I was so embarrassed. I became the butt of the playground jokes, like being called 'microphone head', for months until it grew back. Of course, my mates were on my side and protected me through the bullying taunts, but it was pretty traumatic.

I was never really interested in academic work at school and it didn't come easily to me either. I'd had extra help when I was at primary school but the truth was, by the time I'd started at Hugh Christie secondary school, I just didn't care about maths and English because I wasn't good at them. In hindsight I probably should have been tested for dyslexia because I still struggle with reading lots of text and spelling, but things were different back then and if you found it hard you weren't helped but were labelled thick rather than having what we call today, a neurodiversity.

I always knew if I wanted to have nice things I would have to work for myself but it never really occurred to me that we were poor until I went with mum to clean one of the big houses up one of the long lanes in the village when I was a young teenager.

Sometimes I would go with her on her cleaning jobs to help out, and that was the first time I got a glimpse of how the other half lives. There seemed to be endless rooms in this house with TVs and posh furniture and a fridge full of food. The couple who owned it even had their own ride-on lawn mower. I remember thinking that was so cool and that one day, if I was rich, I would get one for my mansion!

The one thing I was good at in school was sport. When it came to PE, I was a different person than in the rest of my lessons. All the confidence I lacked in the classroom came out when I was out on the running track. From my very first term at Hugh Christie's, it was clear I was the sporty kid. It was evident from early on that I had a natural talent for running.

A lot of my success in sport was down to Miss Page, my PE teacher who was the only person that made me really believe in myself and who told me I could do anything I put my mind to.

She was a tall, strong woman with a warm smile and a kindness that I didn't see in the other teachers. Of course she cared about me doing well in her class but I also felt like she really cared about me as a person too. She'd always be checking in about how things were going in other subjects, how things were at home and making sure that me and the 'gang' were staying out of trouble. It was Miss Page who made me do cross-country even though I hated it, and she put me in the school team to compete against other schools. It was that first race for the team that changed everything – so I should thank her really.

With my big afro, green skirt, white shirt, socks and plimsolls, I actually ran pretty well, even leading with about 20 metres to go before a girl from another school called Stacey overtook me at the last minute and I came second. Oh, wow, that feeling of being beaten hit hard in my stomach and I hated that I lost, even though I didn't even like cross-country. I think that was the moment something clicked in my head. I realised I wanted to be good at something and this set me off on my mission to be the best. I started competing against other schools in the 1500m and won lots of races in my first year. I finally had something I was really good at and proud of.

I think it's really important to call out how special a really good teacher can be to your life, especially for children who come from underprivileged backgrounds. They can give you the confidence and self-worth you need to believe you can achieve your dreams and that's priceless. I feel so lucky not just to have had Miss Page in my camp as a kid but to have her still in my life as a friend now. Every few months she meets up with Kerrie, Lara, Kim and me and we go for walks, paddleboarding or for lunch, talking and laughing about the old days and what's going on in our lives now. I believe those reliable friendships can be the best kind of therapy.

4
—

Dreams Do Come True

WHEN I TALK TO YOUNG PEOPLE AND THEY ASK ME about how I got to where I am today and how I managed to achieve so much success, I tell them that hard work and dedication, self-belief and courage all play a part. But first you have to have a dream, you have to know what you want. It's no secret that opportunities for young people from underprivileged backgrounds can seem out of reach and that's why as a kid from a council estate breaking records and becoming an Olympic hero might have seemed like a pipe dream; but so long as you have that pipe dream there's a chance it might come true.

When I was 12, Miss Page suggested I join the local athletics club, and that was how I found David Arnold. Dave was a retired marathon runner who had to quit because of an injury, but now he was a coach at Tonbridge AC. One day after school Mum drove me over to Tonbridge School; a posh boarding school in town, where they trained, to meet him. We did interval training, endurance training and generally improved my fitness and I loved every minute. The following year I won the 1500m in the Kent Schools Championships and I was selected to represent the county at the English Schools' Athletics Championships in Plymouth, where to my shock, in my first athletics season, I won gold.

That day as I crossed the finish line, I felt that sense of utter pride and glory for the first time. The buzz of winning and achieving something was unlike anything I'd felt before and the more I won, the more I loved it. Soon, while my friends were going out to roller-discos and meeting boys, I was out training every night after school always reaching for that next big medal.

People sometimes ask me how I didn't realise when I was at school that I was gay and I think my athletics training probably had a lot to do with it. While the other girls were busy dressing up and experimenting with make-up to impress boys or obsessing over posters of their favourite member of Duran Duran, I was out running.

My idols were athletes like Sebastian Coe and Tessa Sanderson, not pin-ups like Simon Le Bon. It's not like I was interested in girls either, I just wasn't interested in romance full stop. I assumed it would be something that would come later in my life and as the child of a teen mum, I wasn't in any hurry to grow up too quickly myself.

My first kiss, though, was with a boy called Simon in the trees near my house when I was five years old! His nan and grandad lived at number 58, next door to our first house in Riding Park. But for most of my childhood I was a tomboy.

I lived across the road from Tess and Julie, two girls about my age and although we weren't the best of friends after we grew up, when we were little we used to play doctors and nurses. I happened to always be a boy doctor kissing one of them as a female nurse – all for the storyline of the role play of course. It never occurred to me I was kissing a girl, it was just a game. The Katy Perry song, *I Kissed A Girl* came out too late, otherwise maybe I would have realised what I liked a little bit sooner.

Sex education in schools back then didn't even mention different kinds of relationships, there was no diversity at all, so my options were pretty limited. The 'classes' were just a quick chat about the importance of abstinence and how not to get pregnant as far as I can remember, then we would laugh about condoms. There was certainly no mention of women being able to have a relationship with other women, let alone any other kind of diversity.

In 1988 it became law under section 28 of the Local Government Act that intentionally teaching any kind of homosexuality or publishing any materials around homosexuality in schools was prohibited. I'd left school by then but in the years running up to that, while I was at Hugh Christie's, the silence around homosexuality was definitely already well-established.

For many people in the 1980s, 'gay' was a dirty word and it was used as an insult in the playground and the workplace. The AIDS epidemic had swept through the USA and was now claiming lives in the UK. It was long before the kinds of medical advances that mean HIV is no longer a death sentence and people were afraid of getting it.

Back then I remember the horrifying scare tactics and TV adverts from Public Health with tombstones on them that were made to make you think being gay was the worst thing in the world. Maybe that explains why there was nobody I knew or had even heard of in our community who was gay. It just wasn't something I thought existed in our quiet little corner of Kent, so I never considered it for myself.

What I do know looking back is that I never really enjoyed being with boys. I liked their company as friends but when I went out with a few on brief occasions, I never got that tingly feeling when we kissed and I never was a girly-girl dreaming of getting married. Now I know why! I did have one big teenage crush on this boy called Lee. It was nothing sexual, but he was a pretty boy, and all the girls at school liked him. I soon moved on though because I got distracted by him in an important English Schools race when I was 16 and I realised I liked winning more than I liked him.

* * * * *

Instead of boys, running became my first love. In 1984 as Team GB flew out to Los Angeles for the Olympics the summer after my 14th birthday, my big dream really started to form. I was already winning national medals in school competitions and I'd had a taste of what victory felt like.

My eyes were glued to the TV during the school summer holidays, as I watched Sebastian Coe sprint to victory in the 1500m final that summer and as I watched him collect his medal on the rostrum I could only imagine the euphoria that must have been coursing through his veins. "One day, that will be me," I said to my mum.

I even met Tessa Sanderson the summer after her Olympic heroics winning Javelin Gold against Fatima Whitbread and that had a huge impact on me. Mum and Dad took me and the boys to Butlin's and Tessa turned up in a silver sports car with a javelin along the side wearing her Great Britain white shellsuit, signing autographs. As a black British woman who'd

47

had such huge sporting success, she was a massive inspiration to many. Hearing the national anthem being played for her, Seb and Daley Thompson, who were the three athletics Olympic champions, gave me goosebumps.

But 1984 didn't bring just one dream but two. The second came when our class had a careers day at school and a soldier from the armed forces recruitment office came in to tell us all about the different jobs you could do in the military if you signed up. They spoke about the Royal Air Force, Royal Navy and British Army with such passion and gave out leaflets with the logo 'Be The Best' on them before showing us a video about all the different roles on offer after you completed basic training.

When I heard about the job of Physical Training Instructor (PTI) in the British Army, I was immediately hooked on the idea. PTIs were based at barracks and did basic training like all soldiers but then when they qualified they got to be in charge of the physical training for all the soldiers. Working in army gyms, the job of the PTI was to make sure every soldier was fit and strong enough to do tours of duty for our country, so it was a pretty big responsibility.

Back then, you had to be 17 and 9 months old to join the Women's Royal Army Training Corps (WRAC) and I could not wait. They provided your accommodation, food and uniform and everything you could need, plus they paid you. It felt like it could be my ticket out of sleepy little Hildenborough and give me something to belong to and a sense of purpose that I never really found at home.

"It's perfect for me, I really think I can do it," I told Mum and Dad, full of excitement and enthusiasm when I got home. They were stunned at first because I'd never shown any interest in the army.

My grandad, Mick's dad, had joined the Navy in 1943 because of the war but that was never really spoken about. They were pleased I had a goal, though, and so was I. I felt like lots of doors were closed to me because I didn't have the confidence in my academic ability to go into higher education and I had never even heard the word university! The army seemed like a place where my discipline, hard work and physical skills would pay off, and it wasn't just a job, it was a career.

From that day, while I carried on training with Dave for athletics meets, I also had my heart set on joining the WRAC. Although my Olympic dream was still in the back of my mind I now had one which felt much more reachable. In just three years if I worked hard and got selected I would be able to join up to serve my country and that felt like the greatest honour. Then I could work on the Olympics after that. Once a year from then on I begged Mum to take me to the Army careers office so I could pick up their latest information and imagine my life as a recruit.

When I reflect on the two big dreams I had growing up I wonder whether I would have wanted to continue with them if I'd known the impact serving in the army would eventually have on my life as a gay woman or what being a runner would have on my physical and mental health. I am not sure if I would have felt differently or whether it would have changed anything, but it definitely makes me want to make a difference and change lives for young people growing up and going into those jobs today.

* * * * *

I truly believe that every family has its little secrets – the things no one talks about for fear of rocking the boat or being judged.

Some families have bigger secrets than others and I was pretty young when I realised my family had some whoppers!

One day when I was 16, I went with Mum to Sainsbury's in Tonbridge shopping and we were walking around the aisles when I spotted another young girl with her mum who seemed to be staring at us. Weirdly, in a town full of white families, even though her mum was white, the little girl had black hair and light brown skin just like mine. I didn't think anything of it at first but then when Mum sent me off to pick up some beans from the next aisle I had to walk past them and I heard the woman say to the girl: "That's Kelly."

I literally ran back to Mum, totally confused and told her what I'd heard and asked how the woman knew my name? We walked around and Mum went up to the woman. The girl was just staring at me. I couldn't hear what they were saying but they definitely looked like it wasn't the first time they'd spoken and when Mum came back over to me, she looked cagy. Who were they? I knew from Mum's look she wanted to just finish the shop and get out of there, so I bit my tongue and pretended it hadn't happened while she paid for the shopping, but back out in the car park I confronted her.

"That young girl is your sister, Kelly," she said matter-of-factly. "Your biological father Derrick went to live with her mum Linda after we split up and they had a daughter called Lisa, that was her." Wow! Seriously, that is how I found out about a sister I never knew I had and to make it worse, she only lived six miles away from me!

It turned out that Derrick, who we'd never spoken about for all these years, had another family and was living with them just up the road from me the whole time. And while he basically didn't give a shit about Mum and me, he was living with Linda,

Lisa and her baby brother, Danny. My mind was reeling. It was a huge shock and I felt totally betrayed. I couldn't believe my mum would keep such a huge secret from me for so long, especially when they knew how I felt about being the odd one out in our family unit.

Mum said she was worried I would get too close to him if I met that side of the family and I think she worried he would try to drive a wedge between us but she was doing that herself by not telling me. What I did know is that Linda passed her a piece of paper with her number on. My mum didn't want to talk about it at all but over the next few months I begged and begged her until she finally gave in and arranged for me to go over to their flat and meet Lisa and Danny. Linda said it would just be her and the kids which was actually a bit of a relief, because I was more intrigued about Lisa.

Turning up at the front door I felt sick because I didn't know if the man I have now nicknamed 'sperm donor' would be there! I met Lisa though and we hit it off straight away. Okay, I was jealous of her hair. She had long, defined curly locks unlike my afro. Danny was this cute mixed-raced baby, but I didn't really get to know him for years.

It was a surreal part of my formative years and a lot more went on over the next year, but as I write this, I have been questioning why at '39+14' I'm still trying to piece this together? I suppose it's releasing that childhood trauma. I accept I may now know as much as I ever will about their relationship but I am at peace with my family identity and where I came from and that's really important to me.

After the Sainsbury's episode, Mum and I started to drift apart. I don't know whether it was because of the betrayal, because she seemed to be spending more and more time out of the house or because I was just growing up and moving on but we just didn't seem as close, something that took a long time to heal.

* * * * *

School finished in a flurry of school discos and shirts being signed. I had really bad marks in all my CSEs – quite frankly because schools didn't cater for young people like me who found it hard to concentrate and learn well in a classroom setting – but luckily you didn't need any to join the army.

I'd already run my last English School Championships when I was 17 in Birmingham, winning the 1500m race and, as a result, I was selected by the Olympic Committee to take part in the first mini Youth Olympics Games in Papendal, Holland. I jumped at the chance of going on the ferry with some of the other Tonbridge AC members, it was really exciting, but definitely wasn't glamorous.

The ferry was open-sided with the rain hammering down and the sea was so rough like a rollercoaster, a lot of us were sea sick. But after we recovered, we were ready to go. Mum had made the trip over too.

The feeling of representing my country was something else and when I crossed the finish line first in the 800m race I got a little taste of what it might be like to actually win a 'real' Olympic gold – it was indescribable. I stood proudly on the rostrum in my Team GB kit, a Union Jack draped around me, and the gold medal around my neck. I felt a lump in my throat as they played *God Save The Queen*.

I was still on cloud nine when I returned to Hildenborough but I barely allowed myself to dream I would experience that again. Instead, I focused on my next missions: getting a car and joining the army. First came the white S-reg Ford Escort.

I remember passing my driving test first time, being cocky as I got back, ripping my learner plates off when I was home, telling Mum and Dad that I would treat them to a Chinese takeaway, only to break down in Tonbridge and have to get a tow truck home; how humiliating!

When I was eligible to start the recruitment process for the army, Mum took me to Tunbridge Wells Recruitment Centre, where I filled in an application and had to do an entry test. I didn't score highly because my academic journey through school was so poor. I desperately wanted to be a Physical Training Instructor but I was gutted when they told me the intake was already full and I would have to choose something else if I wanted to join in March of 1988. I didn't want to wait any longer so I looked at the three other options I had and decided to go for an HGV driver course. I liked driving cars, so how much harder could it be in a four-ton truck? Plus, I knew that once I was in, I could try and retrain in another trade if I wanted to.

What some of you may not know is I actually got a sports scholarship to go to Minnesota University. I did consider it but wanted to go into the army so bad that I didn't pursue it. I think now how life would have been SO different for me. Although looking at the weather over there – sod that!

A lot went on when I was 17. I got a job at Princess Christian Hospital working days in the Oast House at the same location where Mum was working nights as an auxiliary nurse. My job was as a nursing assistant working on a ward with men who had mental and some physical disabilities and although it was really hard work it was one of the most rewarding jobs I've done.

I loved helping the patients to do simple tasks like wash and dress and some of them were so sweet I got really attached to them. I was devastated when one of the patients passed away.

It gives me such huge respect for all the doctors and nurses who work in the NHS. During the pandemic I couldn't begin to imagine what they were going through with so many people coming through their doors and passing away.

Then one night the Christmas before I was due to start my basic training, they put on a work party so we could all have a few drinks and I drove there because I didn't drink alcohol. What happened next changed my family forever and I suppose caused a lot of my issues as an adult about trust and drink.

Mum had clearly had a few drinks at the party and when I looked up from playing pool with some of the other nursing assistants, I saw her hanging off some other bloke, kissing him and laughing. I saw red. I couldn't believe what she was doing behind Dad's back, but I also felt like I might cry so I charged out of the bar and got in my car and drove straight round to the house of a guy who I was briefly seeing, which was only a couple of minutes down the road. Suddenly Mum and the mystery guy she'd been with were hot on my heels and came screeching up to the house minutes later. Little did I know he was related to my boyfriend!

"What the hell are you doing?" I screamed, full of anger, dragging the guy out of the car and then proceeding to clamber over to try and grab my mum. She ran off and I think this is where my pent-up frustrations and anger as a teenager came out because I gave the guy a black eye! How could she do this to our family, to Dad, Kevin, Stuart and me?

I rushed home balling my eyes out and told my dad: "She's pissed and you better go and get her!"

Suddenly all the feelings of hurt and abandonment I'd been carrying around all those years came crashing down on me and I felt like the world was falling apart. The one thing I felt bad about was leaving my dad and brothers that night, but I knew I couldn't be there, so I called my best friend Kerrie.

"Come and stay here, Kel, Mum says it's fine," she said. So I drove over in the middle of the night and I never went back to live at home again.

I learnt later that Mum had been having an affair with a guy for a while and soon after she left Dad and the boys. Dad was devastated and I couldn't bear to see him like that after all he'd done for us. The boys were only nine and seven so they didn't really have a clue what was going on. It was only three months until I was due to go off to Guildford Barracks and start my new life, and I couldn't wait to escape. I stayed with Kerrie and her mum until it was time to go. I visited my brothers, dad, nan and grandad but I didn't speak a word to Mum for months. I thought I might never speak to her again.

In March 1988, a month before my 18th birthday, I got the train to Guildford where a load of other new young female recruits were also waiting to start out on the biggest journey of their lives. We piled onto a bus at Guildford station and were taken to the barracks where I would be spending the next eight weeks in basic training. As we drove through the giant gates, topped with barbed wire, I felt my dream was finally coming true and I was beyond excited. I was there at last: Private Kelly Holmes – regimental No. WO804986.

Although it was one of the most difficult times in my life for many reasons, being in the army was massively influential. I still had a really close relationship with the army right up to this month as I have been Honorary Colonel for the Royal Armoured Corps Training Regiment for five years (but I am moving on now) and I'm incredibly proud of having served my country for nearly 10 years.

The army is a place where young people can feel valued, learn trades, be a part of a community, your biggest family, and learn respect and more importantly, self-respect. My journey there was a bit of a rocky one, but it made the things I achieved when I was there all the more rewarding.

5

Fear

A QUESTION I'VE BEEN ASKED AGAIN AND AGAIN since I came out is: "Why now?" Not why I'm gay – I think most people these days thankfully realise that your sexuality isn't your choice, it's part of who you are, as much as your IQ or whether you can sing in tune (I can't, by the way, if you're wondering!). But people do find it hard to understand why I would keep such a big part of my identity hidden away for so long in a world where diversity, inclusion and acceptance are seemingly so prevalent. I remember having to take a deep breath as I clenched my fist and silently dug my nails into the palm of my hand one day soon after I came out when a journalist asked me: "Why do you think it is that you were so ashamed to be gay?"

I have to make one thing clear right here, once and for all: keeping my sexuality private for all those years was never, never about shame. No one ever has or could make me feel ashamed for loving the people I love or living my life authentically. I believe that's my right and even though I may have done it behind closed doors and without other people knowing publicly, I'm proud to say I've always been true to myself and I've never wished I'd been born different. When that journalist asked me that question, I told myself she just didn't understand, smiled and ended the interview as soon as I could. But in hindsight, perhaps if you've never had to live through it, you wouldn't understand.

To understand, you have to know what life was like for gay women in the army in the 1970s, '80s and '90s. While there was never shame for me, there was fear, and a hell of a lot of it. You have to remember that less than three decades ago, the army was a very different place to what it is now.

On our first day, turning up to Queen Elizabeth Barracks in Stoughton, the culture shock was real. There were platoons doing drills on the parade square as senior officers yelled at them. Elsewhere, others were doing physical training sessions with their PTIs – even more yelling. We were shown to our living block which was filled with loads of female recruits. In the Women's Royal Army Corps (WRAC), I only came into contact with other female recruits those first few weeks.

When we arrived, we were allocated beds in dorms of four, on long corridors in the barracks living quarters. All thrown together, all new on the job, we were eager to succeed and pass our training, so we formed an instant connection with one another and all tried to help one another out.

Training was gruelling. We were ordered to run or march for miles on end with our Bergens and seemed to constantly be getting yelled at, though I actually enjoyed the discipline and the routine as well as pushing myself to my physical limits – something I'd learnt to do when training with Dave.

The standards expected in our living quarters were just as

exacting and an inspection from our strict senior officers could come at any time. I quickly learnt to fold the neatest hospital corners on my single mattress and to keep my few belongings in perfect order in case of an unexpected visit.

We each had a small wardrobe next to our steel-framed beds to hang our civvies in and drawers to keep a few personal belongings from home. There wasn't room for much else but it didn't bother me – I didn't have much. Plus, the fewer things you had the easier it was to keep tidy and avoid a bollocking when the senior officers came round to inspect living quarters.

Uniforms were always in line for inspection and that took a bit of getting used to. As well as our trademark green berets, we were given regulation green shirts and combat trousers with long green socks and black combat boots.

The group of girls on my floor would each take on their own role in keeping all of the kit in good nick and we would create a sort of assembly line to make sure each one was perfectly turned out. One person would have responsibility for de-fluffing our felt caps, another would make sure our boots were in order and so on. My job was ironing the shirts. I know it sounds mad but I loved it, and still love ironing now. I would take the creased cotton shirts and starch them so heavily and stiff with two parallel pleats on the back and the crease line on the sleeve razor sharp; they would stand up almost on their own. Then I would hand them out to be hung neatly in each dorm. To this day, I'm a stickler for a well-ironed shirt.

We looked after one another in those first eight weeks of training like we were a family. I have such fond and funny memories of spending evenings sitting on the floor of the corridor outside our dorms, all shining our toe caps with spit and black boot polish until they came up like mirrors.

We would share stories, gossip, talk about home and share our dreams with one another until we could see our faces in the leather. We did fail the odd inspection, but it was fun and I started to feel at home.

My first encounter with a woman was a shock. I really wanted to be able to include her name here as it was a big deal for me starting to understand my sexual identity. After all these years, I didn't even know where she was or if she would be happy for me to mention her. But amazingly, I've managed to get back in touch through the wonders of Facebook and she is happy for me to share her first name: Lynne.

One evening, as we were getting ready for inspection, I went down to the laundry room (the ablutions as they were known) at the end of the corridor where the washing machine and dryers were whirring around and Lynne was in there, sorting her washing.

I'd seen her around of course and we'd spoken a bit in the group with the other girls but now we were alone together, I realised I felt slightly nervous and I wasn't really sure why. She had a pretty face but it didn't really occur to me that I fancied her until suddenly, she leaned over and kissed me on the lips.

I remember having this overwhelming feeling once the shock subsided, that it just seemed right. It was just a kiss but felt so good, so much better and more exciting than anything I'd felt with either of the two boys I'd been out with.

Then I questioned in my head: Am I gay? Yes I must be!

* * * * *

Standing at the far end of one of the dorms, dressed all in black and white with joke-shop goofy teeth, I couldn't stop laughing as I performed the mock wedding ceremony in our barracks.

"Do you take her to be your loyal wedded wife?" I lisped as the girls all broke down in fits of giggles.

I played the toothy vicar while two of the girls stood in front of me, one with a white sheet as a dress and makeshift veil from a net curtain and the other dressed in uniform. It was inspired by the 1988 TV series *The Verger: Tales of The Unexpected*, with Harvey as the groom, Penfold as the bride and Lynne the angel.

We'd pushed the furniture to the sides of the room and lined up chairs in rows for the congregation and everyone was playing along. The two girls kissed each other on the lips, as I announced them wife and wife and everyone was howling. It was just a few weeks into training but just like me and Lynne, another two girls were now seeing one another.

Looking back now, we were so naive to do that and we were very lucky not to get caught because I dread to think what would have happened. But to us it was just fun, we were kids messing around. I imagine those early times were a bit like Freshers Week in university, only without the alcohol.

There's something crazy about your first love, your heart feels like it's about to explode with excitement. Plus it was the first time I'd ever felt really comfortable being that close to anyone. Most importantly, we laughed a lot and our personalities connected.

We were both sporty and it was just fun to be around one another. We were both due to go to HGV driver training after our basic training ended, even though I desperately wanted to be a PTI. Knowing I was going to be with Lynne eased my jealousy towards all the recruits who were heading out on PTI training from our intake.

It turned out she was seeing a guy before she joined up, but she said it was nothing serious, and that it didn't really feel right with him, which makes sense now. I think part of the reason it was so special is because it was all new – our first experience of being in a same-sex relationship.

We had a halfway break in the middle of basic training where we all went home for the weekend. I loved going back to see my family, Dad, Kev, Stu, Nan and Grandad but I missed Lynne like crazy and couldn't stop thinking about her the whole time.

When I got back to the barracks, to my surprise, she had missed me as much as I had her. Remember there were no fancy phones to get in touch, plus I still didn't know what my emotions meant. I thought she might have hooked back up with her boyfriend or something, but it seems she felt exactly the same way.

Lynne told me when we reconnected through Facebook recently: "I remember missing you and thought, 'what is going on in my head with feelings for you?'" It wasn't just us either, there was a girl in my dorm who was going out with another of the girls, so the four of us got close.

I can't remember when I found out and I had no idea there was a law in the military making it illegal to be gay. I didn't know I was gay when I first joined, I was just a teenager who was exploring her sexuality I suppose so learning about the potential consequences seemed irrelevant. Can you imagine losing your career, being jailed or vilified just because of being attracted to someone?

Looking back, those first eight weeks of training prompted conflicting emotions. I felt the most 'at home' and 'right' I'd ever felt but being conscious that you were breaking the law also felt very confusing. I wasn't the only one. I was lucky that there were lots of other girls in my intake who were going through the same thing, working out their identity. We all just knew to keep quiet, keep our inner feelings hidden and protect ourselves and each other as much as we could.

There were simple things we learnt to do, like never addressing letters to female friends or even our sisters because they got vetted by senior officers and they might think we were writing to girlfriends back home. The same went for diary entries. We knew never to use girls' names or to write anything that might implicate us. There was no privacy and anyone could read your diaries at any time.

We had no idea at the time that LGBT+ rights charity Stonewall had already been fighting to rescind the outdated regulations against same-sex couples in the military since 1986, but it was another 14 years before they finally got overturned by the European Court of Human Rights. In the meantime, we just had to deal with the fear of persecution.

After missing Lynne so much on my first trip home, the next time I took her with me. Mum and I still weren't talking and I knew from Dad's letters that she was still seeing that guy. Mum was still living at the house. Her and Dad were living separate lives, which I couldn't get my head around. I guess it showed how much Mick loved her and that he wasn't ready to let her go and that he wanted to keep things as normal as possible for the boys, but it seemed so wrong to me.

When we arrived back at Hildenborough Dad, Nan and Grandad were waiting, all so proud of me and keen to hear all my stories of my time away. I introduced Lynne as my army friend and no one suspected anything different. Kev and Stu can't even recall me bringing someone home so it must have seemed completely normal, even though my heart was racing the whole time we were there.

I kept my distance from Mum and instead tried to just have a nice time. Dad had a new puppy called Charlie and I remember Lynne and I both taking him out for the day. It felt good just to have her there with me. Kev and Stu loved asking endless questions about what it was like to be a soldier. It was nice to go back home to see everyone, but by the end of the weekend I was ready to return to the barracks, which now felt like home.

Back at Guildford, training stepped up a gear as we prepared for passing out. Non-commissioned Officers (NCOs and Senior NCOs) would bark orders at us as we practised marching on the parade square or went on Combat Fitness Tests, which were an eight-mile run/march carrying full Bergens. I loved the challenge. The only thing I hated was swimming because I've always been petrified of water, but with a bit of encouragement from the other girls, by a miracle, managed the obligatory timed one length of a 25m pool without drowning.

I know there were people of colour in the army in my time, but we were very few and far between. There was one mixed-race girl in training but she left before the end of the course. I recently googled WRAC Guildford and I haven't seen one platoon photo of anyone that doesn't have a white face. I know it's a different institution now but it's crazy to think how I was still the odd one out after all those years.

By the time I passed out, Mum had finally moved out of the family home and was living with the other guy so when Dad turned up in the car, he was with Kevin and Stuart plus they brought Kerrie with them too. I was mortified when he showed up and drove his car straight across the parade square. With everyone taking the piss out of me, I felt embarrassment along with horror and the shame – because it was forbidden! But the important thing was that he was there.

Mum came by herself on the train, I thought she looked awful and it was upsetting as I just thought she didn't care. After the ceremony she got the early train from Guildford, so we barely spoke, but I was determined not to let family drama get in the way of my big day. Dad took the rest of us out for pasta to celebrate the start of my journey in the army that changed my life – the best and worst of times.

At the end of basic training you get sent off to do your specialist training or 'trade training' and for me that meant going off for 14 weeks learning to be an HGV driver.

Life at the Army School Of Mechanical Transport was a completely different experience from Guildford with another whole new bunch of people to get to know, including men. At 5ft 4ins tall, I could barely haul myself up into the cab of the monster trucks and had to sit on cushions to make a bucket seat, so I could see over the huge steering wheel.

I remember the words "double the clutch! double the clutch!" being drilled into me. Once we were trained we were sent out of the barracks compound all times of night and day and in all weathers to practise. One night I remember being terrified as another squaddie and I got lost up on the misty Yorkshire moors for hours.

The biggest change between Guildford and Leconfield was that the barracks were mixed and there were way more men than women, which made the atmosphere really different. I got on well with the blokes and I liked their company even though there was so much testosterone around it could be overwhelming. I'd actually found it all a bit odd being in an all-female environment in basic training after being at a mixed school. The fact we were all thrown in together meant there was much more partying and wild nights at the NAAFI, the resident bar for soldiers.

I'd never been a big drinker when I was at school because I'd always put my running first so while my friends had been going out drinking in the park, I'd been at the track doing time trials with Dave. Now I was only doing my HGV training in the day and had my evenings free, I had a chance to get a taste for pints of cider and dancing til all hours to live bands that would come to visit.

I enjoyed that period of letting my hair down. We would all drink and dance and the straight girls would openly hook up with the guys but of course, for gay men and women, the ban was still in the front of our minds. If we wanted to have a snog at the end of the night we would have to sneak off or give each other secret signals. That was the start of a lifetime learning to hide that part of who I was, but I think it was also the first time I realised how much my childhood had affected the way I saw relationships.

The other culture shock on a mixed base was that sexism was also rife and WRACs, as we were known, were often labelled 'dykes' as an insult, even if they were straight. Some of the male soldiers had a saying that 'you're a dyke or you're WRAC so go against the wall and I'll ride you like a bike' which basically meant if you weren't up for sex with them, you were gay. It was a really toxic environment in some ways but I learnt how to make the best of it and quickly became an expert in avoiding suspicion that I was gay by getting on well with the lads or sticking up for myself and others and calling a lad out by shouting, "piss off you tosser!"

You do what you have to do to get by and, when I was that age, I was at the start of the career I'd longed for since I was 14. I just focused on passing my training so I could get my first proper posting.

I knew I couldn't come out properly in the army but there was one person I really wanted to know that I'd realised I was gay and that I was happy, Dad. He had been there for me through everything and still then he was at home looking after my brothers. I decided to write to him.

'The girl who came to stay with us isn't just my friend, she's my girlfriend,' I wrote. 'I really like her.'

A couple of days later, I rang Dad from the payphone to see if he got the letter. I was nervous when I heard him on the line but he just said: "I got your letter, are you okay? Do you want me to come up there, because I'll get in the car and be with you…"

"No, no, it's fine," I said, cutting him off. I didn't want my bloody dad turning up, 'how embarrassing' I thought. "I just wanted you to know that's all. I'll see you when I come home."

"Well, as long as you're happy," he said. And that was that. He didn't need to say anything else because I knew he loved me for me and would support me no matter what.

In the years since, I've realised just how lucky I was to have that two-minute conversation and that kind of support from my dad and then the rest of my family when I finally told them, because so many people I've met haven't had that.

It was only months later when I went home again that I found out Mum had found the letter I wrote to Dad so she knew I was gay too, even though I didn't want to tell her.

"I can't believe you told your dad and not me," she said, when she confronted me. "What did you think I was going to say?"

"How was I supposed to tell you when we weren't speaking?" I snapped, angry that she'd read the letter and I hadn't been able to tell her on my own terms. I hated that she'd gone snooping around for something I wasn't ready to share with her but in hindsight, it was a relief that Mum, just like Dad, accepted my sexuality for what it was and loved me just the same. For all our ups and downs, I will always be grateful for that and when we became much closer again in later life, I let her know how important it was to me to feel that acceptance.

I think because I'd already had the feeling of rejection from such a young age – it was more important than ever to feel safe and that I wasn't going to lose the people I cared about in my life.

One thing that still makes me so sad today is when I hear stories from people in the LGBTQIA+ community, as it's known now, who haven't had support from their families, or who have even been totally disowned. I've seen people disowned by their families, and for what? Embarrassment, anger, shame?

I know it's complicated and the emotions can be difficult and overwhelming when someone you think you know is different from who you thought, but you can't underestimate how devastating and damaging it can be to reject someone for something they had no choice in, and that they can't change. It would be like disowning your own child or brother or sister for having the wrong colour eyes.

If anyone is reading this now, and doesn't know how to react to a relative coming out, I would say the only answer is to listen and learn. Educate yourself and remember that the person you love is still the same person, it's who they love that makes them seem different or as I say 'unique'. No matter what's happened with my family over the years I always felt that love and security and I don't think I'd be here without it.

* * * * *

Sadly the end of the HGV course was the end of my whirlwind romance with Lynne. We both got posted and we ended up drifting apart. I was sad to be honest because I had been happy at that time, but that's what trying to have a relationship was like in the military, always moving around – even harder if you were hiding everything.

Anyway, I did commit to my training and after 14 weeks I was a qualified HGV driver and was transferred to 17 Port and Maritime Regiment at McMullen Barracks, Marchwood, near Southampton, to work with the Royal Electrical & Mechanical Engineers (REME) under the then 53 Port Support Squadron, as a driver transporting stores to and from the port to the barracks and other places.

The worst part was the 7am start in the morning but I had plenty of spare time in the evenings and this time living in the barrack accommodation blocks, I had a brilliant group of friends around me who made it so much fun.

It was the end of 1988 and Acid house music was taking over the nation – clubbers partying all night with bright yellow smiley faces on their t-shirts and neon glow sticks. We were no different on the barracks and we would often take a small open boat from Marchwood Port to Southampton docks to go out in the bars and clubs.

I never did any drugs but I loved that feeling of totally letting go, dancing and singing with all my mates to the deafening music. It was the complete opposite of the discipline and order that we had to follow back at the barracks. I still love having a good dance now on a night out, it's one of those things that helps you feel totally free – and I don't care who's watching!

It was while I was at Southampton that I did start to secretly explore my sexuality outside of the barracks. I remember one day when I was in town, standing in the newsagents and seeing a gay magazine. I can't remember what it was called but it was mainly men, and I know that I stood in the shop flicking through the pages with my heart racing in case anyone spotted me. I was too scared to actually buy it in case it got found by anyone, but I managed to look up where the gay bars were in Southampton in the directory section and memorise their names.

One night, a few weeks later, I made my excuses and disappeared out into the night all on my own. I figured that if I went as a Civvy and anyone else from the barracks was in there it would mean they were gay too so we wouldn't blow each other's cover.

In dungarees, Kickers, a Paisley shirt and bright red lipstick, I walked up to the entrance of one of the bars I'd read about and went in. It was called Brannigans. I've since found out it's now a branch of Lidl but at the time it felt like one of the most exciting but scariest places on earth. The adrenaline was pumping as I walked through the smoke, with Black Box's *Ride on Time* and *Pump up the Jam* by Technotronic playing.

"Can I have a lemonade please?" I asked as I stood at the bar. I didn't like drinking on my own and I wanted to keep my wits about me too in case anyone asked where I'd been later.

I stood there and looked nervously around the room and just saw loads of couples, all looking so comfortable in their own skin as they drank and laughed. I suddenly felt totally out of place and I was far too shy to approach anyone to talk, but I did see a woman walking towards me and panicked, so I downed my lemonade, and made a swift exit into the night and back to Marchwood. It felt like a total anti-climax at the time but it was my first ever trip to a gay bar and, when I look back, I'm proud of myself for going. I am laughing at myself as I write this – oh, the memories.

After that, though, I decided to stick to having fun with the other girls in my accommodation block. There were quite a few guys who fancied us and a pair of twins in particular who took a shine to me and would always be competing for my attention. I used to enjoy winding them up, by kissing and flirting with them.

In the girls' block we all used to hang out of the bedroom windows singing Chaka Khan's *Ain't Nobody* into our hairbrushes at the group of lads that would gather down below. Even though I didn't find any of them attractive, it felt good to be part of the fun. Unlike Guildford, as far as I knew most of the girls in my block at Marchwood were straight, so I wouldn't have had much chance with them anyway!

Not getting involved in any serious relationships also meant I was able to concentrate on my career and, by complete chance, I got my first opportunity to chase my dream of becoming a PTI. The barracks itself had no female PTIs so when me and the other girls turned up, even though we did the Physical Training with the guys, there was no one there to take female sports like netball, rounders and hockey (what makes me laugh now is that we were never even allowed to try football and rugby).

I loved the assault courses and circuit training and generally keeping fit so I would train in the gym a lot. One day, I asked Ray, the sergeant in charge, whether I could take the girls for PTI. I explained I'd passed the intake test but that the course had been full so I'd done my trade training as an HGV driver but my ambition was still to retrain in physical training.

To my surprise he said yes and I started putting on training, matches and tournaments for the female soldiers and they loved it, we had such a laugh.

One of the PTI Warrant Officers at the gym was none other than the 400m hurdle athletics star Kriss Akabusi. He worked at the gym but then would disappear off for weeks on end to do training for one competition or another and I found out he was competing for Great Britain in the IAAF World Cup and for the army in the Inter-Service Championships.

Hearing him talk about his training made me think back to training with Tonbridge AC. He asked me to go along to see him and Roger Black at Southampton AC where they trained and I went down a couple of times. I was reluctant to do too much, though, as I'd made a conscious decision to give up competitive running when I joined up and my main focus was on getting onto a pre-selection course for my PTI training.

6

E.N.D
(Effort Never Dies)

IT'S NO SECRET I HAD A DIFFICULT CAREER WITH more than a few setbacks before I was finally crowned double Olympic champion but I've always believed those failures along the way made me stronger. I believe that rule is true in all areas of life, not just running. I didn't do well at school and I believe failure is your greatest teacher. It all goes back way before my professional athletics career and started when I was in the army.

Everything seemed to be going in the right direction at Southampton as I trained the other girls in the barracks and mixed with the other PTIs. I never experienced the luxury of moving out of the dorms so having my own private room as a perk of taking fitness classes in the morning, at lunchtime and in the evenings, was fab. Ray – the PTI in charge on a day-to-day basis – and Kriss did some research to find out when the next pre-selection course in Aldershot, Hampshire for new PTIs was,

and sure enough, in 1989, I was off to take the course. I was devastated when it all came crashing down. I was told they didn't think I was suitable for the nine-month course I would need to pass to get formally qualified as a PTI.

They said I was physically strong enough and could run but my coordination skills let me down, as well as my voice which they said wasn't loud enough to bark the orders. "You should be shouting from your stomach and not your throat," one of the female PTIs said.

Back at Marchwood, even though I failed, the office for the army athletics team had found out about me competing in the Youth Olympics and asked me to join their team to compete in the Inter-Services Athletics Championships. I really didn't feel like going back into competitive sport but I thought if I did that and was successful they might give me another shot at the PTI course, so I signed up, and finally took Kriss up on his offer of training down at Southampton AC.

I was out of practice to say the least but I soon got back in shape with hill runs and time trials and I was selected for the team to compete against the RAF and the Navy. At the championships in Cosford later that year, I won both the 1500m and the 800m and started to make a name for myself in army athletics.

When someone tells you you are not good enough, you can either give up completely or want to prove them wrong. The latter is what I did, getting permission to go on every course I could that would teach me more skills so that I could learn to umpire, coach or referee.

At the end of 1989, after my string of successes and a trip to the rehab centre in Headley Court for a knee injury, another PTI selection course came around and this time I was on top fighting form, and cruising through onto the nine-month training programme.

April 23rd, 1990, was the day my first dream came true. I'd wanted this moment since I was 14, I was now just turned 20 at Army Physical Training school in Aldershot, home of the British Army. I enrolled on WRAC course 81, with 20 female soldiers, two of whom were from Brunei.

We were all various ages, plus there were two senior NCOs and a captain. It was to be a pivotal part of my life because it finally gave me the identity I had been craving, and a chance to be a leader – to show everyone what I was made of. The accommodation we lived in was 10 Coy (company) Duchess of Kent Barracks; a women-only barracks, and it was back to the days of sharing rooms.

I shared with two other girls. I wasn't seeing anyone when I went on my course, but I worked out a few were gay just by using my 'gaydar'. What you have to remember is it was still like a shared secret, sometimes you knew but you didn't need to say and that's how it was. It's very hard to describe but there was an unspoken understanding. You're going through enough shit on a course like that without worrying about dobbing somebody in for being gay, so I felt comfortable enough.

Although I wasn't actually seeing anybody on my PTI course, I probably kissed a couple on drunken nights out. Drinks seemed to be something that we did for fun up in the NAAFI but I never really took those things seriously because we were just young and enjoying ourselves. I think everyone has gone through those stages in life.

There were different phases of this course. The first phase we were all together and it was probably the best phase for me as it was all about our fitness at the PT school. We were then split up into groups and joined up with guys for the second part of the course. That included a trek up Snowdon in Wales, which was hell because of the unbearable weather. But despite that, I actually enjoyed being with the lads because you were pushed harder and I always wanted to hold my own with them.

There were different girls leaving throughout the course either through injury or being taken off for being too quiet or not making the standard. It was always hard to see them go as they had become good friends by now.

* * * * *

By the time we went back to 10 Company in Aldershot for the next phase, I was still loving it but this is where my career was turned upside down totally unexpectedly. I remember this part of my past in particular because I failed this section of the course – and you know by now how much I hate failure. Basically, for some reason when it came to the assessment for this part of the course, I was pulled aside by the commanding officer along with four other girls.

"You need to buck your ideas up," she told us. "You're not going to pass if you continue like this."

Inside I was devastated but I wasn't going to allow anything to get in my way, so I trained even harder. By the time we got towards the end of this section and after seemingly being whittled down, I remember getting called into this room. One of the officers was on my left and the other one straight in front of me, telling me I'd failed. I was devastated and they wouldn't give me the reason or what I had done wrong.

"If you're going to fail me I want to know why!" I demanded, totally losing it in front of the officers, something you are not allowed to do. "You've had it in for me from the start and

I want to know why." But it was no good, I was simply told I wasn't going to make it through the course but that they would encourage me to continue in the army and stay on the athletics and cross-country team. That made me even more angry – they were happy to shatter my childhood dream without giving any good reason but they still wanted to keep face so that I would win them medals for the army. I was not happy.

I will never know why I was kicked off that course. Was it because they found out I was gay? Was it because I was mixed race? I have no idea but what I do know is it was humiliating, it was embarrassing and no one could give me an answer. What I did do was go back into the barracks and trashed my room. I have just been reminded of that as I write this now.

I couldn't face going back to Marchwood a second time or going back to being an HGV driver. If they weren't going to let me fulfil my dream I decided it was time to say goodbye to the army. I was due to go home on leave before the last part of the course anyway, so I packed up my things and went to the personnel office and told them I was going to leave.

"I don't know what I'm going to do, everything's ruined," I told Dad back in Hildenborough. "It's the only thing I want to do."

He tried to comfort me but there was nothing anyone could really say to cheer me up. I went round to visit Mum. Things were still pretty bad between us because now not only had she had an affair but she'd got married to the guy in secret without telling me.

It was as though she hadn't wanted to tell me because she still felt guilty for what she'd done – too bloody right in my opinion. But I missed her and I was feeling so low from failing to pass the course, I thought seeing her might make me feel better. But back at the house, there was another shock waiting for me. There was a message from the Army Training Centre in Aldershot asking me to call them back.

"You need to get back to Duchess of Kent Barracks," the officer in personnel told me when I rang up. "We'll explain everything when you get here but we want you to continue on the course."

I couldn't believe it, the rollercoaster wasn't over yet! I couldn't understand what had happened, the commanding officer had been so clear I wasn't good enough to carry on, but I wasn't going to pass up an opportunity to get back on the course, so I packed my bags and got on the train.

The rest of the girls were now in Wales on the last phase of the outdoor adventure course and they were as shocked as me when I walked back into the dorm two days late, ready to join back in. They were pleased to see me – even they thought it was mad that I'd been let go. No real explanation was ever given for what happened. I was simply told by the Lieutenant Colonel, another officer who outranked the Commanding Officer, that they wanted me back on the course and would just judge me on my performance going forward. I never had anything more to do with the officer who booted me out and I heard not long after that she'd left the PT course team.

Finally I qualified as a PTI and earned my stripes as a Lance Corporal. I was moving up in the world so I didn't allow myself to think about why I'd had such an awful experience – until years later. Now, I'm convinced my failures both at the pre-selection course and on the PTI training course were more than just bad luck.

I was fitter than most of the other women in the group, had experience and was even winning medals for the army and yet two women wanted me out. I've gone through my life saying I've never experienced racism because of the colour of my skin but looking back, while I haven't suffered racial abuse, I can't help wondering whether the fact I was the only mixed-race girl on the course meant there was some discrimination involved. It's horrible to think that about an institution that you love but there has been some bad history of discrimination. In any case, I wasn't going to let anything hold me back any longer. I'd been rubber-stamped as a PTI and I was ready for whatever life threw at me next.

I was also pleased when Mum turned up to see me passing out to the next level of my military career as a PTI. She came with her new husband and their new baby, Penny (my youngest sister). We had grown apart a bit by now but I think maybe it was her way of showing me that no matter what else happened in her new family, she would always love me.

In my later years, I came to realise that although they were stressful and turbulent, those first four years of my life before Mum met Dad and we formed our little family unit, were something really special that she would never share with anyone else. She had three other children with two different fathers but I was the only one who had ever been on their own with her.

My first posting as a PTI was at Imphal Barracks in York, also the home of 2 Signal Regiment and later 21 Signal Regiment; it was just a wonderful place. I love York with The Shambles, Cathedral and city walls and I always think that one day I'd go and live there. I lived upstairs in the Elizabeth block which was not far from the Military Transport section, where I used to go and visit the HGV crew because I still had a connection with the drivers.

I met a girl at those barracks and actually lived out for six months with her, it was really secretive, and there was a huge amount of pressure so it didn't work out and I came back.

I loved being a PTI but it was about to become a very different army because in 1992 the WRAC disbanded and that meant that all the women would be spread out around the different military units, rather than a big congregation of women at certain barracks. During those times it was very difficult being a woman and making decisions about careers and changes.

York barracks was amazing though and I met a load of guys who I was competing in the army athletics team with. I still had the dream of being Olympic champion and I remember watching the Barcelona Games and seeing Lisa York, a girl I'd beaten as a junior in the 3000m and thinking, 'I could do that'.

When I was posted there and after winning an Inter-Services cross-country, there was a guy called Wesley Duncan, who had coerced me to get back into civvy athletics. Luckily for me, he was based in Ealing which was straight down the motorway from Beaconsfield in Buckinghamshire, the location of my second posting as a PTI.

7
—

Raided

I WAS IN GREAT SHAPE DURING MY TIME AT
Beaconsfield, as I had plenty of opportunity to train alongside
work. The PTI job was everything I hoped it would be and any
worries anyone had about my voice not being loud enough were
blown out of the water as I was soon ordering platoons of men
over assault courses and around the track. Being a corporal and
having PTI status, I was respected and had certain privileges,
like my own bunk. I didn't go out a lot and had saved up for
a TV with a VHS recorder in my room which I would use to
watch videos that we passed around the barracks.

One night I was passed a video that had been recorded off the
TV. It was a documentary about a gay male couple who wanted
to adopt a child. It was the early '90s and even gay marriage
was a distant dream in the UK, so it was totally unheard of and
everyone was talking about it. I don't think I was given it because
anyone thought I was gay, it was just something so unusual that
everyone wanted to watch – and I had a video player.

I had mixed feelings watching the show because I'd always assumed I would never have children because of my sexuality, but maybe the world was changing and it would make me feel differently. Even though I love children I've never had a strong maternal instinct – yet it was eye-opening to see how the world on the outside of the army bubble was gradually starting to change.

Life inside the army, on the other hand, was very much still in the Dark Ages and my most traumatic experience happened at that same barracks in Beaconsfield. One morning I got a tip off that the Royal Military Police were sniffing around, back on their mission to seek out anyone in the barracks who might be gay or bisexual.

I'd spent five years looking over my shoulder, never getting into deep conversations with anyone I didn't know well or revealing too much in the NAAFI or at social gatherings. It was well known that the RMP would dress in civvies and get talking to men or women they thought might be gay, then try to lull them into a false sense of security and encourage them to either flirt or confide in them about their sexuality, so I was always on guard. Sometimes, though, they resorted to aggressive and violent bunk raids that left soldiers terrified.

When our barracks got the tip-off that the RMP might be staging raids, I got that same sense of panic I'd had in basic training when the senior officers would come to do random inspections, but now it was much more intense. I remember my heart pounding as I scrabbled around my room, checking every drawer for anything that could give the remote impression that I liked girls.

I gathered up my letters from Kerrie and Lisa and my diaries and put them in a box, took them out to the car park and put them in the boot of my car. Then all I could do was wait. Nothing could have prepared me for the onslaught when the RMP burst into my room.

"STAND BY YOUR BED!" one of them yelled as two others stormed in and started turning everything over.

"You're gay, aren't you?" he went on. "Admit that you're a lesbian!"

I stood physically shaking as two men and a woman went through every one of my belongings, pulling out drawers and emptying them out one at a time, throwing all my clothes out of the wardrobe onto the floor and trampling all over them as they flipped my mattress and steel-frame bed upside down. They brought my wardrobe crashing to the ground to check behind it and went through all my bags and personal belongings. The only way I can describe it is like when you see prison cells being raided on TV. That was how it felt – as though I was a prisoner who had done something terrible and they were there to intimidate me into admitting it.

Just as they started pulling all the furniture away from the walls to check for hiding places, my heart jumped and I felt like I was going to be sick.

I realised that in the rush to clear out all of my belongings I'd left one thing – the VHS of the gay male couple was still in the video recorder. I knew if they found that I would be done for, that would be it. Any little piece of evidence they could seize on would be grounds for discharge. I could lose everything I'd worked so hard for.

I could feel my hands trembling as I watched the search, just waiting for them to hit play on the recorder but by some miracle they didn't.

They found nothing and left my ransacked bunk to move onto the next poor soldier. I felt my heart beating out of my chest as I tried to calm myself down by taking deep breaths. I was a wreck and I started shaking and crying.

The whole experience was terrifying, and yet I knew it was coming, so I couldn't begin to imagine how I would have felt if I'd been caught off guard. 1993 in particular is now known as being one of the biggest military 'witch-hunts' and it is estimated that over 300 service personnel in the military were targeted by RMP because of their sexuality.

It's memories like that which have stayed with me all my life and which instilled such fear into my core as a 23-year-old and made me unable to live my life openly. I wish I could send a message to those people who raided my room that day. Even though I know they were only doing their jobs – and of course it's the government and authorities who were mainly to blame – those individuals caused such trauma to me and hundreds of others.

The thing that hurts me the most looking back is the way I was treated like two different people. On the one hand there was Corporal Holmes, the champion athlete PTI who won medals for the army to be proud of, and trained hundreds of men and women to be the best version of themselves for their roles and careers, physically and mentally; and then on the other hand there was Kelly Holmes who they treated like a second class citizen if they even got an inkling that I might be gay.

It made me feel like a commodity to them that they wanted to use, and then turn on if I didn't follow their draconian rules. Only now do I realise the post-traumatic stress I suffered as a result of having such a mentally damaging relationship with the army.

Thirty years later, whilst looking into the injustice of the Military LGBT ban, I met a woman who was actually discharged after her own RMP raid at the same barracks 10 years before me. Hearing her talk about the fear, shame, horror, abuse and interrogation that resulted in her discharge brought the trauma flooding back and I had to have counselling to deal with it because it was so painful.

Hearing Jean's story made me feel like this was my sliding doors moment. She has never had a good quality of life and her mental health has been hugely affected. I now know, of course, that there are many other former military personnel who suffered and I hope, with the justice that came in the summer of 2023, that others have been able to get closure too.

8

One Track Mind

DIFFERENT PEOPLE REACT DIFFERENTLY TO TRAUMA, as I've learnt through my many hours of therapy over the last couple of years. For me, throwing myself into my work, goals and challenges and keeping busy has always been key to getting me through. People sometimes ask me why I move at 100 miles an hour and never sit still, and that all goes back to me using it as a coping mechanism to stop me thinking too much about things that had hurt me. After the RMP raid, I threw myself back into my job as a PTI and athletics as a way of giving me a focus. If I was training and competing I had less time to think about the raid, my sexuality or relationships with other girls in the barracks.

Now training with the wonderful Wes – as I now called Wesley – he encouraged me to take part in a UK championships and, to both our surprise, I won it and recorded the qualifying time for the World Championships in Stuttgart. I used my leave to compete in Germany because I was not allowed time away, being only one of three PTIs in the gym I was in charge of. I have great memories of Stuttgart, breaking the English record for the 800m in the semi-final but not qualifying for the final, and watching Maria Mutola, who was to become my nemesis, training partner and biggest rival.

In between training for the World Championships, I was still working full-time at Beaconsfield and a camera crew was sent to the barracks to film me running PT fitness sessions. The footage shows me yelling at a platoon of male soldiers as they scramble over and under wooden logs on an assault course, and running with them round the track.

It was weird to think that the army was so proud of me and so keen to publicise my great achievements and my Olympic hopes when, behind the scenes, I was being raided by the RMP and held under suspicion by senior officers over doubts about my sexuality. I wondered what Sean Bean, who narrated the documentary, or the thousands of viewers who watched it would think about the fact the army's new athletics star had almost been given a fail on the PTI course or had my bunk ransacked during a raid.

Going to Stuttgart one minute and then patrolling the barracks the next was a bump back down to earth but I loved the fact I was a soldier and also a good athlete, as they went hand in hand, and I was fulfilling both my childhood dreams – not many people could say that. I stayed in Beaconsfield until the beginning of 1994 and then ironically got a posting to Aldershot with 251 Signal Regiment as their PTI. Back to Duchess of Kent barracks that had been the scene of so much grief. I was now juggling both my army career and my athletics after doing so well at the Worlds, but there was one thing missing from my training schedule.

Since I joined the army I'd totally lost touch with Dave but I knew if I wanted to take running seriously again, I was going to need him in my camp. He was the only one who knew how to keep me going and make me improve all the time. I wrote him a letter out of the blue asking if we could talk about my training and he invited me down to see him so on my next leave I travelled down to Tonbridge.

"What's your ultimate goal?" he asked me. And for the first time I think I said it out loud: "I'm going to win an Olympic gold medal." We both laughed and just like that we were back together again.

Dave would come to Aldershot to train me and occasionally at weekends I went to Tonbridge to train with him. I went on to win gold in the 1994 Commonwealth Games in Victoria, Canada, silver in the European Championships in Helsinki and bronze in the European Cup at home in Birmingham and I was really starting to make a name for myself outside the military, but I was still a soldier.

One minute I was running for England or Great Britain, the next I was umpiring a rounder match or taking PT. I spent the next couple of years doing both and still went on in 1995 to win World Championship silver and bronze in the 1500m and 800m respectively. We didn't have long before the 1996 Atlanta Games, so if I was serious about achieving my goal I was going to have to up my game – and get some backing from the army. I applied for leave to train and ended up having a more flexible role with the Army Youth Team so I could concentrate on running.

Getting selected by Team GB for the Atlanta Games in the summer of 1996 was an incredible feeling and I think Dave and I both felt like this was going to be it. The whole country seemed to get behind me too. The impact on my mental health after the Beaconsfield raid didn't come out for years after because I was concentrating all my energy on the Olympics, but I definitely felt like I was only of value to the army because of what I could do for them and that wasn't a nice feeling.

I was so proud to be a part of the army and to serve my country so I never questioned it sooner but I think I knew all those years ago just how desperately change was needed and I promised myself that if I ever got the chance, I would help to bring that change about.

* * * * *

I always knew the Atlanta Olympics in 1996 would be one of the most significant milestones in my athletic career, but I never could have predicted the reasons why. As I prepared to compete in the 800m and 1500m events, I took on a rigorous training regimen that pushed me to my physical and mental limits.

I knew from the start that preparing for the Olympics required dedication, discipline, and a relentless pursuit of success and it wasn't something I was going to take lightly. After all, everything I'd done in my life so far was a challenge and I hadn't given up yet – I wasn't about to start now!

My training schedule was intense, with gruelling track sessions, strength training, and endurance workouts. Each day, I pushed myself to the limit, striving to improve my speed, endurance, and overall performance because I knew everyone else who was qualifying would be doing exactly the same thing.

Under Dave's guidance, I followed a meticulously planned training programme of interval training, long runs, hill sprints, and technical drills to enhance my speed, agility, and race tactics. The training sessions were physically demanding, but

I embraced the challenge, knowing that every effort was a step closer to achieving my Olympic dreams. I also knew that if I was to get anywhere near winning, it would also require mental fortitude and resilience, so I started working closely with sports psychologists to develop mental strategies to cope with the pressure and expectations that come with competing at the highest level.

Visualisation techniques played a crucial role in my mental preparation. I would imagine myself crossing the finish line, feeling the surge of adrenaline and the sense of accomplishment like I'd felt in other races in my career. They said it would help me build confidence and belief in my abilities, enabling me to perform at my best when it mattered most.

As the summer of the Atlanta Olympics drew closer, the antic-ipation and excitement grew. I knew that this was the pinnacle of my athletic career, and frankly, I felt in better shape than I'd ever been. There was a real feeling that this was going to be my moment and I was determined to make the most of this oppor-tunity. Some army guys saw me off at the airport and I was on my way to Atlanta.

In the days leading up to the Olympics, things started to take a turn.

As I flew to Tallahassee to the holding camp where the rest of Team GB were preparing, I noticed a bruise on my left shin and a shooting pain as I ran on it. I went to the team doctors who did a scan and discovered I had a small stress fracture in my leg.

"You need to go home," one of them said.

"Do I have a choice?" I said, exasperated.

"Yes but you risk breaking your leg completely."

There was no hesitation. "I'm running," I replied.

I was devastated and called my mum who told me to come

home but I wasn't about to throw away all the hard work I'd put in to get there so I just changed my training schedule to keep the weight off the leg as much as I could by cycling and training in the pool instead of on the track. With the support of Dave, my medical team and their unwavering belief in my abilities, I remained focused on my goal but there seemed to be much more risk involved now.

Eventually we moved to the Olympic Village in Atlanta and I got to share a room with none other than Tessa Sanderson, the 1984 Olympic champion who I'd met all those years before on holiday with Mum and Dad at Butlin's. I couldn't believe I was now finally going to be competing for my country just like her and inspiring another young generation of kids back home like me.

Stepping onto the track in the Centennial Olympic Stadium was a surreal and exhilarating experience, despite my anxieties over my injury. The atmosphere was electric, with the world's best athletes gathered in one place, ready to showcase their talents. The weight of the moment was enormous as I wore Team GB's red, white and blue, but I embraced it, knowing that I had worked tirelessly to earn my place among them. I told myself I deserved to be there just as much as everyone else.

Astonishingly, I got through the heats and the semi-finals. As we lined up on the starting line for the 800m final, I felt a mix of nerves and excitement, no one expected me to get this far running with a stress fracture but as the race began, I was purely focused on executing my race plan, relying on the countless hours of training and preparation that had gone into this.

Just before I went out, I was given a pain-killing injection into my leg which hit the bone. The pain was excruciating. Somehow, though, I found that my mind took over and I was there running. As I pushed myself, giving it my all, I felt a sudden agonising dart of pain shoot up my leg – because I had only done my last couple of weeks' prep in the gym and pool, I ran out of gas. I ended up in fourth place at those Games, only being pipped to the line by a tenth of a second which, given the circumstances, was pretty incredible really.

I was still totally gutted as doctors and physios rallied around me, packing and supporting my leg, and taking me off to the medical room. Stupidly, what a lot of people don't know is that I also doubled up at those Games running the 1500m as well and getting to the final but hobbling around in 11th place. People have said I was crazy. Looking back, I was!

It was a long time before I would find the courage to return to compete at that level but in hindsight my journey to the Atlanta Olympics was a testament to the dedication, sacrifice, and resilience required to compete at the highest level. While my appearance at the Games did not go as planned, the experience taught me invaluable lessons about perseverance, mental strength, and the ability to bounce back from setbacks.

Atlanta served as a stepping stone for future successes and fuelled my determination to achieve Olympic glory. It was a reminder that setbacks are not permanent, but rather opportunities for growth and learning. That summer will always hold a special place in my heart. It was a pivotal moment in my career that shaped me into the athlete and person I am today.

I also realised that if I really wanted to continue and fulfil my Olympic aspirations at the next Games, I needed complete focus. I loved the army but it was time for me to turn my attention to running full time.

So I wrote to Lieutenant Colonel McCord, the Chief of Staff responsible for granting leave and discharge to soldiers who wanted to pursue excellence in other areas. She was also the officer who got me back on my PTIs course.

Ma'am,

Following my personal disappointment in relation to my results at the Olympic Games and the overall results of the British Athletics Team in Atlanta, I have carefully analysed the situation.

My individual events were dominated by Russian Svetlana Masterkova, who won both the 800m and the 1500m Olympic titles. Masterkova, like the majority of Olympic champions, carefully and ruthlessly prepared for Atlanta by isolating herself from everything in a single-minded quest to win at least one Olympic gold medal.

Both Masterkova (although she is Russian she resides in Spain during the winter and spring) and Michael Johnson, an American who won the men's 200m and 400m, are ultimate examples of this method of preparation.

I am positive that with the right preparation, both mentally and physically, I can beat Masterkova at this year's World Athletics Championships, which will be held in (*ironically) Athens during August. My wish is to go to South Africa at the beginning of February, returning in May. I would spend a period of time in Pretoria at altitude and then Stellenbosch in the Cape to finalise my preparations at sea level.

When I return from South Africa in May, I will immediately enter into a carefully structured competitive programme which, coupled with training, will lead me to win at Athens.

Unfortunately, we live in a world where success is the only criterion, and I believe I can win a gold medal in Athens, but this will entail me embarking on the programme I have outlined.

I would be grateful if the Army would consider my needs and my aim to become the world's first number one middle-distance runner.

I am Ma'am,
Sgt K Holmes
WO804968

I was delighted when the response came and I was given the time off to pursue my running career. It felt like I was able to pursue my two great loves in life at the same time. Plus, Pretoria in South Africa is the perfect climate and altitude for athletics training so when I had the chance to travel over with Andy Norman, one of the most influential men in British Athletics at the time, and a few other athletes including Fatima Whitbread, the world champion javelin thrower, I jumped at the chance.

A small group of Brits were going to take part in the ABSA Games in 1997. One of the races was in a University town called Potchefstroom which had amazing training facilities, a beautiful sunshine climate and a lovely old town centre with traditional architecture and wide, tree-lined streets. It was a million miles away from Hildenborough but I loved it.

South Africa in the '90s was an exciting place of change, with the release of Nelson Mandela and the abolition of Apartheid and I enjoyed learning about the history of it all. I felt completely at home there in a way I didn't think I would. In fact, I soon set my heart on one day buying a house so I could train there whenever I wanted. By June, though, I had to return to the UK for an Army Athletics team performance.

My wins in civilian races and my travels around the world had given me a new confidence and the army no longer had the same hold over me that it once did. I decided there and then it was time to sever my ties once and for all. I went over to Lieutenant Colonel McCord who had been so accommodating in allowing me to go and train in South Africa and said: "I think it's time for me to part ways with the army for good."

She wasn't happy to see me leave but she could see that if I wanted to achieve my true potential as a civilian athlete I couldn't have the distractions. I think she could also tell by then that I'd lost some of my respect for rank from spending so much time outside the institution, so she saw it was time to go.

I was just a few months off ten years of service when I left and I still remain really proud of that time in my life. When I received my final report, Lieutenant Colonel McCord described my conduct in the army as 'exemplary'.

Of course I was proud to have such a glowing report from my time serving the Crown but I couldn't help wondering at the back of my mind how things could have been so different.

It made no sense to me that I could be praised so highly on my performance as a soldier but that something so personal as my sexuality could have led to me being discharged with disgrace. The main reason for leaving was so that I could focus on my career but I would be lying if I said I wasn't relieved by the fact I would never face the fear, degradation and humiliation of being raided or investigated by the RMP ever again.

* * * * *

After Atlanta I convinced myself that if 1996 was rock bottom, 1997 was going to be my year. Now I was free from my army responsibilities, I could focus completely on my Olympic dream and that meant first going to the World Championships in Athens that summer. From there it would be a straight shot towards the Commonwealth Games in Kuala Lumpur the following year and then the Sydney Olympics in 2000.

I moved back home to Kent so Dave and I could go back to training in Tonbridge just like we had for the five years before I enrolled in the army. While I was serving, I'd saved up pretty much all my money. When I wasn't working, I was off training or competing, so I'd been able to put down a mortgage on a house in Sevenoaks – a three-bed ex-housing association semi with a garden.

It was the perfect base for me to do my training again and it meant I could spend more time with Mum, too. We'd never spent much time together since she remarried and had Penny but I liked being around her more. I would go round to her house and take her dog, Harley D, named after Harley-David-son motorbikes, out for long runs and sometimes Mum would come on her push bike too, which was mainly a distraction and disaster as she was so slow!

Dave and I started training sessions with a couple of other athletes from Tonbridge AC so they could help me keep pace and, to begin with, things were going well. I was in the best shape of my life, unbeaten so far that year and I was running times that were well on track to get me a medal at Athens.

Having beaten the British 1500m record earlier that year, I was five seconds faster than anyone else in the world and was far and away the favourite to win. But a few weeks before we were due to travel over to Greece for the World Championships, my ankle started niggling again.

At first it was just a twinge but then as I continued training a shooting pain would come and go. "I'm worried," Dave told my physio Kevin Lidlow. "I think we need to do something about it now before it gets any worse." I tried to stop myself

Childhood memories As the only mixed-race girl, I was always placed right in the middle of the school photo! (Top) with Mum and baby Kevin and (above) with my afro and school friends Lara, Paul and Kim

First love Lynne with Charlie the dog, Kev and Stu

Wife and wife I played the toothy vicar in our mock wedding ceremony

Service Proudly wearing uniform (top) and pictures from my PTI course

Holmes truths Family is everything. They are the people who love you

Natural talent Hair slowed me down but I still won the English Schools at 17!

'Sarcastic but fun!' Sarah would become my longest relationship

Through the pain barrier Rupturing my calf, ironically in Athens, in 1997

First Olympic medal Celebrating winning bronze in the 800m in Sydney in 2000

True love With my two dogs Whitney and Barney

On track for success Gold at the Commonwealth Games in Manchester in 2002 (left) and silver in the World Athletics Championships in Paris in 2003 (right)

Golden feeling The look on my face says it all as I cross the line in FIRST place in 2004 in the 800m (above). I use this image now in my motivational speeches and it always gets a great reaction. (Right) doing the double! The same celebration after I make it two Olympic golds in Athens with victory in the 1500m

Homecoming Paraded on a double-decker bus with my two gold medals from Athens. The press cameras followed my every move as I worried about what they might uncover

National treasure Mum enjoyed the scenes as I returned to a hero's welcome. But the paparazzi and reporters soon found out where I lived and it was time to move house

On the Parky show They said I flirted with Tom Cruise – little did everyone know...

Special night Being named BBC Sports Personality of the Year in 2004 was one of the best things to happen to me after Athens

Saying goodbye Waving to the crowd after my last competitive race in Sheffield in 2005

from panicking too much. After all, the pain was only coming and going and I only needed it to stop long enough for me to get round the 1500m race. But I was also determined not to end up in the same situation I faced in Atlanta, so I booked to see the best specialist in Europe at the Institute of Sport in Munich.

Dr Hans-Wilhelm Müller-Wohlfahrt told me the stress on my Achilles tendon was causing the pain and gave me two injections to try to ease it. Nothing could have prepared me for the pain as I hobbled out of the clinic on crutches. I called my mum from my bedroom that night in floods of tears as the agony in my leg felt like it would never end.

"I think he's made it worse," I cried. "What if I can't run at all now? What if the same thing happens again?"

Mum knew how devastated I'd been by my injury at Atlanta and she hated hearing me so upset. It wasn't the first time I'd called her in the early hours of the morning, consumed in pain and worry, but this time it seemed worse than ever before. Just having her there for me on the other end of the line was the biggest comfort and I believe it actually brought us much closer together.

"Everything will be okay, we all love you and we're so proud of you," she told me. And somehow that was just what I needed to hear. It was a huge reminder to me that no matter how much success I had as a runner, I always needed my family and friends around me. My successes were a team effort and I'm very lucky to have had them and others around me through all the ups and downs of my life.

By some miracle, I woke up the next morning and the pain was gone completely. When I landed in Greece I felt fit as a fiddle and wanted nothing more than to get myself back on track with a big win at Athens.

I woke up on the day of the first heat feeling good and ready for the challenge. Lining up at the start, I told myself not to push too hard and to save myself for the semi-finals. I just had to do enough to get through. But after the second lap I could feel myself running erratically, then suddenly, as I took one step, I felt something that felt like an explosion in my leg and an excruciating pain burst through my body, causing me to leap into the air and yelp.

When I came down, I couldn't go another step and I had no choice but to hobble off the track and drag myself to the railings. My mind was spinning and the pain in my leg was like a searing hot poker being pushed into my calf. I couldn't believe it was happening again; first my Olympic dream in shreds and now my World Championship goal in tatters too. It seemed so unfair, I was devastated.

After I had hobbled down the track to get to the end, the medics and physios rallied around me again but this time it seemed the problem was even more serious. They told me that I'd had treatment on my Achilles tendon and had weakened it, causing it to tear as well as rupturing my calf. It meant the muscle had torn apart, causing intense pain. It was going to take a long time to heal.

I left Greece on crutches and heartbroken. Looking back, what I understand now is that at that time in my life, I put all my value and self-worth in how I performed on the athletics track. I think that's because I couldn't allow myself to live authentically in my personal life but also, because I had a hangover from never feeling good enough, I had this constant need to push myself, sometimes to my detriment. A lot of other athletes when they fell on hard times had partners to support them or could relax between training and competitions by going out and meeting new people, but because of the way the military ban on being gay had become hardwired into me, I was always so scared to relax and I didn't go out much. My entire life until then was trying to prove I could be good at something, all triumph and disaster was dependent on how well I did in my athletics career. Another failure like Athens was a brutal blow to my self-confidence.

Back home on my sofa after a couple of weeks of treatment in Zurich and my leg in a plaster cast, I began to question everything about my life and even wondered whether I could come back from the pain, injury, heartache and humiliation of Athens. I should be known as the world champion and instead I was getting known for my terrible luck and repeated injuries. Perhaps being convinced that I would one day win a gold at the Olympics had been completely naive. Maybe I just wasn't good enough.

I wish back then I could have told myself I would return to Athens seven years later and see all my dreams come true.

9
—

Relationships
and Rumours

HOBBLING ALONG THE PATHWAY TO THE CARAVAN, still on my crutches as the other girls carried my bags, I tried my best to put a brave face on but I felt awful. So much for 1997 being my year... My big plan of leaving the army to pursue athletics full-time had fallen flat just months later. All the training in South Africa, breaking the British 1500m record in Sheffield, all seemed to pale into insignificance after my performance in the World Championships in Athens and what was worse, I wouldn't be able to train again until my ruptured calf had properly healed.

A couple of girls, one from the army I had a brief relationship with, knew how hard I'd taken the blow and when I got home they said I should go with them down to Chichester in West Sussex for a week's holiday. It was better than sitting at home on my own reliving what had happened, so I agreed to meet them down there. Claire told me to meet one of her friends called Sarah who I'd never met before at Victoria Station as she was travelling down too. As the other two were a couple I just assumed she was gay and I was right. I know now that they were trying to matchmake us but the setting couldn't have been less romantic – me with my crutches and feeling distraught from my loss, her probably wondering why I was in such a bad mood as we both travelled by train together.

Then the morning after we arrived, things got even worse. We woke up and switched on the little telly in the caravan and it was just rolling news.

"Princess Diana has been killed in a car crash in Paris," the newsreader was saying. "She died in hospital after a collision in a tunnel."

We couldn't believe it, and all started to cry from the shock. The Royal Family was especially important to us having pledged to serve the Crown when we joined the army and back then Diana wasn't only a princess but the biggest celebrity in the world. We watched for hours as the news came out bit by bit, that she'd been chased by the paparazzi when leaving the Ritz hotel with her new boyfriend Dodi Al Fayed, and he was also dead.

It was just so sad to think of Prince William and Harry after all they'd already been through with the public divorce of their parents. I think we had a special love for Diana because of what she did for the gay community during the AIDS pandemic in the late '80s and early '90s too. We sat around comforting one another and reminiscing about her for hours that day. It certainly put things in perspective and I started to try to make the most of the holiday.

Sarah, who worked for the MOD and army but as a civil servant, started to really hit it off with me and by the last night of the holiday we were making plans to see each other when we got back home.

We decided to meet up in London, as she was living in Croydon at the time. After chatting I went home and wrote in my diary that she was 'sarcastic but fun', which I think she'd agree with!

We started seeing one another. It was to become the longest relationship I've ever had. I only had one rule and I made it clear from the beginning: "I can be in a relationship but I can't come out publicly, and I never will, so if that's what you need we shouldn't do this." Sarah was cool with it and I knew she was trustworthy because she worked for the army too and could face discipline if anyone found out about her, so we were kind of safe with one another.

I think the key was that we got on so well as friends and she understood just what was important to me. She never complained about me having to be off training or competing, she just wanted the best for me. I loved her company and within a couple of years, she moved in. Sarah was such a strong person and a strong character who didn't suffer fools. You wouldn't want to get on the wrong side of her but I quickly realised she was incredibly loyal and would do anything for the people she loves.

We would bicker like an old married couple. I knew 100 per cent that she had my back all the time and that's what relationships are meant to be about. I knew she also understood when I got my first dog Whitney and my next, Barney, that she came third in the relationship. It was my athletics, the dogs, then her! She took it amazingly well.

It felt good to have my own little family unit for the first time since I'd left home at 17 and now I was with Sarah, I found it easier to come out to other people close to me. She gave me the confidence to feel like it didn't matter what they thought. Up until I was 27 and left the army, Dad was still the only person I'd told I was gay. Mum had found out by mistake of course but that was it, apart from my fellow soldiers who were keeping the same secret.

I decided to tell Kerrie and Lisa together when they came over to meet me at Mum's house one night when Mum wasn't there. It actually wasn't anywhere near as big a deal as I thought it would be. We sat there chatting and I just came out with it: "I'm gay and I'm in a relationship with someone."

They both looked totally unsurprised and smiled at me. I think they were just really happy for me that I'd found someone. They got on really well with Sarah too. They didn't want to belittle my big moment back then but they've since told me they suspected all along anyway. The same with my brothers, who by now were 17 and 20, running about with girls and getting into their own mischief – they weren't bothered either.

We soon had a tight little circle of friends and family in Kent who knew and accepted our relationship and after all the drama of the army and the trauma of the raids, it felt good for a while. I met Sarah's parents Shirley and Alan and her sisters Sandra and another sister, who all became a part of my family.

Sandra even moved in with us for a while before she went off travelling to Australia. They both kept my secret from the outside world and I just felt grateful to have found someone who accepted me for who I am, and that I could be with people I could trust. Life was good. When I look back at the last book I wrote, not long after I retired from athletics, I get a twinge of sadness that I referred to Sarah as a 'close friend' and covered up our relationship by saying that she and Sandra both lived with me.

I suppose I wanted people to think we were housemates rather than in a relationship. That's just one of the things that makes me so grateful for the fact I can now live my life freely but, more importantly, tell the truth about the amazing friend Sarah is to me now, 25 years since meeting. Never once did she break my trust.

Despite 'being in the closet' as it gets described when you are not freely out, I have had several relationships since Sarah. Unfortunately, for a lot of reasons, things have not always been great and they haven't ever lasted long. I have gone out with people because of circumstance and convenience rather than any great lightning-bolt love-at-first-sight. Sometimes they were sporty so I thought we had a lot in common. I also got attached because I wanted to share my successes with people and the thought of always being on my own scared me. But the truth is, with most of them, we should never have been together.

I wish in hindsight I hadn't rushed into things so much. What I do know and admit is that being with me was not easy.

Most of my partners developed an inferiority complex because of my successes, felt invisible because of my commitment to my work or didn't like the limelight. Most of the time, after the initial buzz of being with me wore off and the reality set in, things didn't end well. More often than not was the realisation that I wasn't going to be coming out for them, getting engaged or slowing down my work to spend more time with them. In my defence I have always been totally honest from the start of every single relationship. I told them: "I am not out and not planning to be and will never come out whilst in a relationship."

I haven't been in touch with most of my exes for many years and out of respect I'm not naming them or putting any details about them here because I no longer know their circumstances. I wish I had been strong enough to have been on my own because maybe it would have been better than an unhealthy relationship.

The problem, deep down, was that I never thought I would be able to come out. Even if they said that was fine to begin with, sooner or later it would start to put pressure on the relationship and eventually they would take it as me being ashamed of them or unwilling to give them the commitment they deserved. As I said before, it was never about shame, but I was definitely still scared of the impact having a public same-sex relationship would have on my life and so I invariably chose my safety first.

One thing I'm comfortable with is that I was always completely open with anyone I started a romantic relationship with – it was cards on the table from the start, even if I thought it would scare them away. As it turned out, a combination of my issues with going public about my sexuality and the unresolved childhood trauma that left me scared of abandonment meant that for most of my adult life relationships were pretty disastrous!

Lots of my closest relationships haven't been sexual. I have had some really long-term friendships as well. Kerrie and her mum Sandy who I adore, Lara and Kim my school buddies, Tess who lived across the road from me, Pat who was my hairdresser, and Flo, Jackie and Emma who don't live close to me but I have known for so long now.

There can be a price to fame that is not always great. I had two friends in particular in my life for years who I fell out with. With one, I think we just grew apart and as our own lives changed and different people came into them which caused friction, we just went our separate ways. Another I felt betrayed by; I felt they were using my kindness and financial support for personal gain.

I am disappointed and hurt at losing both of them, but it's all part of life I suppose. All of us will meet people who will come and go throughout our lives, it's the ones who are meant to be in it that stick around.

* * * * *

Since my appearance at Atlanta, even though I didn't win, my name was getting better known and there was more press attention around me. For some reason the one thing everyone was interested in was my personal life, which definitely filled me with anxiety. I'd gone from one homophobic institution in the army to an industry where there wasn't a single openly gay athlete that I knew of, so there were no role models I could turn to.

Of course there must have been other people, like me, who were keeping it secret, but it was never something that was spoken about. Instead I just kept myself to myself and never allowed anyone to get too close to me. I hated the idea that anyone would start asking me about my home life, my relationships or who I fancied. It was just too uncomfortable.

Back home in Kent I felt like the Only Gay In The Village and I wasn't really on the gay scene. Another saving grace for me when it came to publicity about my private life was the great friendship I had with Jason Dullforce. Jason was the same age as me and we'd met a few years earlier at an athletics meet in Manchester where he was also a middle-distance runner competing in the men's 1500m. A tall, mixed-race guy with long eye-lashes and delicate features, we looked quite similar and got mistaken for brother and sister when I was serving, which made us laugh and we hit it off straight away.

Over the following years our careers had crossed paths many times so we'd got to know one another really well and even our families became friends. So, when the press and other people in the athletics community started to assume we were together romantically, I never did anything to stop it. We'd become really close friends and before I met Sarah we'd spent lots of time together but despite the rumours, our relationship was never physical. I suppose in many ways it was convenient for me to allow people to think we were together and he never did anything to shut down the rumours either. I was always honest with him and when I got together with Sarah he was really happy for me but still neither of us openly denied our relationship, which took some of the pressure off me in the early days of my more public career.

When you're trying to win medals and titles and achieve personal bests and break records you need a kind of single-mindedness that helps you to succeed so if you're worrying about someone finding out about your sexuality all the time, that's a distraction that could put you at a disadvantage if you're not mentally strong.

There were more than 20 openly gay athletes in Team GB in the 2020 Olympics in Tokyo so things are definitely changing but other sports like men's football and rugby are still way behind, which is shocking in this day and age.

My coping mechanism was to completely separate my two lives. I had my little house in Sevenoaks with Sarah, Whitney and Barney and then there was the other me, who was on the track, a sergeant in the British Army and a representative for our nation on the world sporting stage. I felt lucky to have both but I wish in hindsight I'd been able to allow the two worlds to collide.

The other impact of the divide was that I often found myself choosing between the two worlds and inevitably, I always chose running. I was open with Sarah from the start because I needed to succeed in my Olympic dream, perhaps now more than ever after the disappointment of Atlanta. Plus, for the outside world it was a distraction from my personal life. I think all of my life I've strived to succeed so there would be something I was known for. If there was something interesting to ask me about in my career or my successes maybe people wouldn't ask me about my relationships or my personal life. No one could judge me for my love of running.

10

Triumph and Disaster

THE UPS AND DOWNS OF A CAREER AS AN ELITE athlete are like a being on a rollercoaster. Somehow once you get past the nausea and fear of the twists and turns, you're back to craving the adrenaline and having another go. With two pretty disastrous events behind me in Atlanta and Athens it would have been easy to give up or let the mental impact of my injuries stop me from trying to reach my goal. But the same Kel that fought to the bitter end to get onto a PTI course and who managed to get through the trauma and fear of 10 years in an army that criminalised my sexuality decided to fight on beyond the world championships and set her eyes on the next goal.

The fact was, if you looked at my performances when I was at peak fitness, I was the best middle-distance runner in the world. I truly believed that all I needed was for my peak form to coincide with the right races and all my dreams would be achieved.

First I had to undergo surgery on my leg to remove the scar tissue from my injury so it wouldn't affect my ability to get back to peak fitness. It turned out to be an injury that has plagued me all my life and I even had to have another op on it a couple of years ago.

The surgery went well and gradually, with the help of Kevin and Dave, I was able to put more weight on my leg, although running was out of the question. I had to do aqua-jogging (or water running as I renamed it) in the pool – something I hated because I still had my fear of water (I absolutely hate cold water) – and gentle walks to get my mobility back. Anyone who knows me knows I'm always on the move, dashing from one place to the next and never sitting still so it was really frustrating for me to have to slow down and just allow myself to heal. But I wasn't going to do anything to risk going backwards so I followed doctors' orders.

I used the spare time I had to arrange a school sports tournament in Kent called the Kelly Holmes Schools Challenge. It was my first attempt at giving something back to kids who might be like me when I was at school – good at sport but not much else! I got 25 schools involved and they all had to compete in loads of different games.

I funded the whole thing myself so I got pretty creative with the props and the challenges involved. I even managed to get hold of a supermarket trolley for one event where they had to push their teammates up and down the school hall, dunking their heads in the flour, then water, to get the apples. I loved going along to watch all the kids have such a great time mucking in and getting involved with sports.

It was another opportunity for me to spend time with Mum too. She was now a single mum living alone with Penny who, being 19 years younger than me, meant that I never really built a strong relationship with at this time. Her only income was a couple of cleaning jobs so I decided to get her to help out with the admin side of things and she loved it too. She got really involved in setting up all the challenges and we had such a laugh, it was exactly what I needed to take my mind off my injury.

It was many months but eventually my ruptured calf was on the mend and I was able to get back to training at a high level and, with the Sydney Olympics now on the horizon, I was totally focused on getting a medal. But first I had to get in shape for the Commonwealth Games in Kuala Lumpur in Malaysia.

It turned out the key to that was marathon runner Paula Radcliffe. I'd got to know her a bit in Atlanta and I knew she'd also had injury problems so when she told me she'd been to a physio in Ireland who she called "the man with magic hands" I had to go and see him. It turned out she was right and as soon as I started seeing Gerard Hartmann, everything changed.

I flew over to see him in Limerick and stayed close by, working on my injured leg. Within six weeks, I was running again – really running. It was an absolute miracle. I started seeing him in May 1998. I could not get ready in time for the Europeans that year, but with the Commonwealth Games on the horizon in September, that became my focus. By the time the new season started in August, I was back on track. I managed to win my first couple of races of the season which really boosted my confidence and by the time I jetted off to Malaysia for the Commonwealth Games, Athens seemed like a distant dream – or nightmare!

The 1500m was always going to be a tight-run thing with

my two main rivals Jackline Maranga and Naomi Mugo from Kenya in peak condition and me only just back from a massive injury. If I could even just make it round the track in a good time it would be a huge improvement on Athens.

I got through to the final and, on the day, as I gritted my teeth and pushed myself to the limit, I won a silver medal. Just months earlier it was unthinkable that I could achieve such a performance. I was so pleased and it was another medal in the bag.

Having Sarah's support during those first couple of years was invaluable and I will always be grateful to her for that. She was always there, looking after me when I was injured then as I started to recover, looking after the house and Whitney and Barney when I was able to go out training again.

The sad thing looking back was that when I was given the huge honour of being awarded an MBE for my military services, Sarah couldn't come with me. I imagine if I'd been straight and been in a relationship and living with a man, I might have taken him along to Buckingham Palace to meet the Queen when I accepted the honour but, of course, that was out of the question.

There are so many things that gay couples miss out on for fear of scrutiny or being outed before they're ready. I've tried to make sure in more recent years that I take Sarah to more events with me because I think she missed out on a lot when we were together. Over the years, having such a close friendship – and because she is my ex – has caused a lot of problems with other relationships I have had. But she has always been there for me – still sarcastic but a great friend!

It was still an amazing experience getting my MBE. I took Mum and Dad with me and they were beside themselves with pride. Mum in particular – how could she, a single teenage mum from a council estate in Kent be joining her daughter at Buckingham Palace to accept an honour? She was so proud and excited. I bought a new cream suit and a navy hat from a shop on the high street and a local limo driver offered to look after us for the day, driving us to and from the reception.

As I was introduced as Sgt Holmes, Prince Charles asked me why I wasn't in my military uniform. I told him I didn't have to wear it since I had now left the army to become an athlete. It probably would have been better if I had worn my uniform as I hate the pictures of me in what I wore. I didn't have much style and I found that one thing about being secretly gay is I never wanted to show too much personality or draw too much attention to myself. I always thought if I went with the kind of steampunk fashion or androgynous outfits and edgy hair-styles that appeal to me now, I would stand out too much. It's probably crazy because I'm sure no one gave two hoots what I was wearing but I always thought there was a risk someone would think I was making a statement or just assume from my style that I was gay, so I kept it as vanilla as possible. There are tons of pictures I look back at where I hate what I look like.

Still, there aren't many people who can say the now king asked them about their outfit!

* * * * *

In the year 2000, as we started a new millennium, the European Court of Human Rights finally lifted the ban on homosexuality in the British Armed Forces. There was a landmark ruling after initially four services personnel fought for justice having been dismissed from the the military on the grounds of their sexuality.

The court ruled that an individual's sexual orientation had no bearing on their ability to perform their duties effectively. It said that the armed forces rely on teamwork, trust, and cohesion, and excluding qualified individuals based on their sexual orientation undermined these essential elements. This marked a change to the future of LGB rights as the ban had been in place for decades and the institution was being dragged into the 21st Century with the rest of the world.

It was a massive milestone in the fight against discrimination for people like me. But I'm sorry to say I had no clue it had even happened. Astonishingly, the story wasn't widely covered in the mainstream media like I'm sure it would be now. Although I spoke to friends from my army days, none of them mentioned it to me, so I had no clue. There was no letter sent out to former soldiers to tell them, it just happened quietly behind closed doors. For me, life went on unchanged.

I was busy training for my next Olympics in Sydney later that year, so I missed out on any sense of relief I'm sure I would have felt from the ruling had I known about it. It was only years later that I realised the ban had been lifted and, even then, there was no information available about what would happen to a soldier who was found to have broken the law before homosexuality was decriminalised – so my fears of retribution remained and I continued to live my life behind closed doors.

What could have been a year of great celebration became pretty bleak as my training for Sydney was once more blighted by injury. A damaged femoral nerve meant I lost all sensation down one side for about five months. It was better than being in excruciating pain but I couldn't believe my luck that it was happening again. It seemed I was just prone to injuries which would knock my training off course at any moment and make everything feel so uncertain. I would lie awake at night willing myself to heal and get back on track but the more I felt the mental impact, the harder recovery seemed to be.

Gerard was able to work his magic again and I flew back off to Potchefstroom to train with some other British and French athletes who were also going for selection to their Olympic teams. While I was there, I sustained another injury. A 12cm calf tear! I thought my Olympic dream was over but I made selection for both the 800m and 1500m based on all my other years of success at major championships.

The team flew out to the Gold Coast at the end of August three weeks before the opening ceremony in September and the camaraderie in the team was amazing. We trained in parks with wallabies and koalas and the whole experience of being in Australia was different from anything I'd experienced before. Andy Graffin, one of the Tonbridge AC guys I'd been training with back home also qualified for the 1500m and I made friends with Kate Howey, a judo player, who was in the team too, so l often relaxed by watching her train. I think in all my Olympic appearances, she was actually the only other team athlete I watched win a medal.

The relaxed and positive vibe in the team really helped me and in those last couple of weeks before the Games opened, my form improved massively. A few days before I was due to run, I was out on the track with Dave and ran one of my fastest times of the season.

I took home a bronze medal in the 800m that year which was a really big achievement given the setbacks and the fact I only had six weeks of running. The rest was about adapting and using the gym as a way of staying at my peak both physically and mentally. Plus it was my first Olympic medal, so I was on a massive high.

I was so happy that I actually messed up the 1500m as I took my eye off the ball. I remember my coach being really unhappy with me as he thought I had let myself down when I missed out on a medal. But the bronze felt like a gold medal at the time. It was enough to prove that I had it in me. If I could win bronze against the best middle-distance runners in the world after the season I'd had, imagine what I could do if I was on form.

The other big landmark that year was my birthday. The actual day, April 19th, I was training in Potchefstroom, so I'd been out to a karaoke bar with some of the other athletes. It was the most bizarre place, themed like the Wild West and I got up and sang Whitney Houston. I didn't drink as an athlete but that night I got really pissed as I was so distraught about turning 30!

Back home in England, Sarah arranged for a night out in London at a posh Spanish restaurant with Lisa and her sisters and, of course, my best buddy Kerrie. We had the best time and Sarah even booked a limo to take us home to Hildenborough afterwards. I felt rather posh for a girl from a council estate.

People sometimes ask me why I never had any friends or family with me at the Olympic Games like some of the athletes but the truth is I always thought they would be more of a distraction if I knew they were out there in the crowd. Not only because I would be focused on them watching me but also because if Sarah came out, I was paranoid the press would start to latch on to the idea we were more than just housemates. I couldn't have that worry distracting from my performance. It was much easier to socialise with other athletes while I was out there as it was only about sport and then come home to my friends and family to celebrate afterwards.

I would always take a few weeks off from training after every big race and Sydney was no different. When I got home to

Hildenborough I spent a few weeks chilling on the sofa with Sarah, Whitney and Barney, visiting Mum and Dad and eating all my favourite naughty foods like Chinese takeaway and chocolate. The medal was the best reward for all my hard work, but that was a close second.

* * * * *

As an over-thinker and a perfectionist, one thing I do after every race, win or lose, is look back and analyse what went well, what went wrong and how I could have shaved off those few precious seconds that could make all the difference. I also do it in my personal life, which is probably less effective, but for athletics, it really works.

After Sydney there was one clear obstacle besides my injuries that meant I won bronze and not the Holy Grail gold medal I'd been dreaming of all those years. That obstacle was Maria Mutola from Mozambique, who took gold. Maria was an absolute legend in her home country, treated like a queen and a national hero as she'd been winning races internationally for years, putting them on the map for athletics.

I'd been coming up against her in races for years, since she won the 800m in the first ever world championships I qualified for, in Stuttgart. But now she seemed to be on top form and I knew that if I wanted to be the best in the world, I needed to be better than her.

Maria was two years younger than me and if I was going to get to the next Olympics in Athens I would be 34 years old – past retirement age for many runners – so I had to keep in shape. I knew Athens would be my last chance and it was never too soon to start my journey.

One thing that brought Maria success, I was convinced, was

the climate of her home country where she could train all year round. I loved training in South Africa but staying in hotels and renting houses for short bursts in the run-up to big tournaments was disruptive and expensive so in 2001, after my post-Olympic slobbing around break, I headed out to Stellenbosch, with the idea of buying my own place so I could train there for more of the year. Dave and I rented a place to begin with while I trained, but I started looking at apartments to buy.

A disappointing performance in the World Championships in Edmonton, Canada, later that year due to having chronic fatigue syndrome a few months before, convinced me even more that I needed to focus on getting back on top form, mentally and physically. With selection for the Athens Games coming round in three years, this was my last chance to really go for it and come home with gold, or forget my dream forever.

A gold medal on home turf at the Commonwealth Games the following year in Manchester and a bronze at the European Champs two weeks later only spurred me on further to believe I could do it at the big one in Athens, but experience had taught me that it wouldn't come without a fight.

Sadly, that fight meant making some difficult decisions.

Firstly, I made the hard decision to move to Potchefstroom full time, leaving Sarah, my family, and Whitney and Barney behind.

It wasn't just that the climate and conditions and facilities were better for training but also because I'd realised it was impossible to focus on the enormity of my dream when I was living back home in Hildenborough.

When you have a partner and a home, it's too easy to get bogged down in sorting out the house, or cutting the trees in the garden or getting into discussions about things that just don't matter. It sounds harsh but I needed that single-mindedness without outside influence or distractions. Yes, it was selfish but I believed, to be Olympic Champion, I just needed to focus on myself.

"We'll never see you!" Mum said when I told her I planned to move for the foreseeable future.

"I'll keep the house here and I'll be back to see you all," I reassured her. "I wouldn't just leave Whitney and Barney would I?!" Plus Sarah was still living there.

While I was in the process of moving to South Africa, I made another big decision. After decades working together I decided to part ways with Dave and get a new coach. It was after a competition in Crystal Palace, at the end of the 2002 season, when I got chatting to a guy called Jeff Fund from Maria Mutola's team. Jeff was her race agent and manager and the ex-husband of her coach Margo Jennings.

He told me Maria had started training with Margo in Johannesburg just an hour away from where I decided to buy another house. I still had my apartment but the house would be in Potchefstroom at altitude whereas the apartment was at sea level being in Stellenbosch. I figured if I wanted to be the best – and beat the best – I needed to train with her too. Dave was completely against the idea of me training with a rival and said he was worried it would mess up my own training schedule but I was determined.

Maria was so strong, confident and without any self-doubt. After all, she had never been injured and was the queen of the 800 metres. She had years of experience behind her and was pretty much unbeaten, so she wasn't about to be bothered by me training with her. In many ways I thought it would help to have a competitor around.

So, after a conversation with Jeff and Margo, she agreed. A few weeks later, back in South Africa, I travelled from Potchefstroom to Johannesburg to join her for her training. It was one of the most gruelling things I'd put myself through, with hill climbs at altitude and relentless reps according to Margo's exacting schedule. At first I felt downtrodden by the fact I was struggling to keep up but I knew it was now or never. I could give up and go home or I could be as focused as Maria.

Two weeks into training, I spoke to Margo on the phone. I explained to her the problems I'd had with injuries and what I was finding difficult in the training sessions with Maria. She said she could help me and train us both as long as my goal was still the Olympic 1500m title. So I told Dave it was time for us to part ways. Of course he was disappointed and I was sad too but I had to give myself the best possible chance.

Sarah flew out to meet me in Cape Town. I just couldn't concentrate at all. I knew we needed some time together but as she tried to tell me about what was going on at home, all I could think about was getting back to training.

"I'm really sorry, I have to get back to Johannesburg," I blurted out suddenly halfway through her trip. "It's just I have this training schedule I need to keep on top of and it's really tough at the moment."

I think I knew, as I packed up my bags and left to go back to our training base, that was the death of our relationship. Sarah stayed with a friend in Cape Town and when we spoke on the phone I just remember saying: "I need to stay. I need to stay in South Africa. I can't do this. I have to do this one thing. If I don't, that's it, the dream is over."

It was the most selfish thing I've ever done and I knew it wasn't nice for her, seeing me choose running over her but she always knew from the start that was my dream and I think deep down she knew that was how it would end.

Sarah flew home and stayed in my house for six months while I stayed in South Africa but then I needed to rent it out, because I needed to get some income to cover the mortgage, so she went with the dogs and stayed at my dad's until she got on her feet. Once again it was Mick to the rescue!

I started staying with Maria in the house she owned in an affluent residential suburb of Johannesburg called Bryanston, and training with her every day. We became close friends. I even cooked a full Christmas dinner with all the trimmings for Maria, Margo and another athlete, Agnes.

Within a few weeks of starting our joint training, I started to feel much better about my chances of getting into peak form in time for one last shot at the Olympics. But other people in the athletics community didn't like me training with a rival and soon the press got hold of the story that I was holed up in Johannesburg with Maria, having severed ties with my British coach – and they didn't like it either.

Soon stories started coming out in the British and South African press about Maria and me 'growing close' and 'living together'. It was very clear the insinuation was that we were in a relationship and that was why we were training together. One paper carried a headline asking: 'Is this the friendship that went too far?'

I was really pissed off to be honest. I'd left home to get away from all the distractions of my personal life so I could concentrate on training and now the papers were trying to make that into some salacious story. They even said Mutola and I were so close that we decided to 'carve up' our winnings in races in the run-up to the Olympics which was ludicrous, completely untrue and could have got us both in trouble. Firstly she would NEVER let me beat her!!

There had always been rumours about my personal life since I stopped being seen so much with Jason and I knew some people probably assumed I was gay, having been in the army and now a professional athlete with no apparent partner. But there was nothing between Maria and me except for camaraderie in our training and friendship.

The articles made out we'd shacked up together when I was actually still going back to Potchefstroom at the weekends and on training breaks, I was only staying with Maria for ease while we carried out Margo's demanding schedule. Plus, we weren't even on our own most of the time because another runner, Agnes Samaria from Namibia, had joined us to train too and she was also staying at Maria's house. But the papers conveniently neglected to mention that…

11

Black Dog

THE RUMOURS ABOUT MARIA AND ME AND THE split from Sarah took their toll on me to the point where now it was even more important for me to make sure it was all worth it. I didn't want to have made the sacrifices I made only to find myself in another spiral of injuries, disappointment and feeling like a failure. The pressure I put on myself as a result was immense. I guess when all your eggs are in one basket you have to make sure you make it work, otherwise it feels like it will all be for nothing. And when you're focused on a single goal, it's easy to forget all the great things in your life outside of that goal; you hang all your hopes of happiness on it.

Despite my best efforts, after just a few weeks back training in South Africa, the worst happened. Injury struck again. The pain in my leg came screaming back and the physio diagnosed me with something called iliotibial band friction syndrome, which was basically a long complicated name for muscle rubbing on the bone in my knee. If you can't imagine how painful that was, I can tell you it was like fire burning through my leg with every step I took. My injury curse was back and this time I was thousands of miles from home and my family, single again, and had only my competition for company.

The very last thing I wanted was for Maria to see the weakness in me, so I put a brave face on it and carried on. Training was agony and I had to stop every 20 minutes because the pain got so bad I thought I was going to pass out. I laughed bitterly at the fact the press thought I was off gallivanting in South Africa, having some love-in with Maria when, in reality, I was crumbling.

With every training session I had to finish early, as I watched Maria carry on and go from strength to strength, my mental health was spiralling. By the summer I was distraught. This time no amount of physios or chiropractors seemed to make any difference and I was getting desperate. I don't know if you've ever seen a dream slipping through your fingers, but that was what it felt like and I was in a constant state of anxiety.

Despite my worrying state I clung onto the schedule for dear life and when Margo and Maria went to Font-Romeu in the French Pyrenees to train for the 2003 World Championships in Paris, I went too.

We stayed in an apartment with Margo's husband Bobby outside the town centre but while Maria was able to take advantage of all the perfect training conditions I couldn't even get out on the track. I was stuck in the pool again, trying to get the strength back in my leg. The only time I went to the track was to cheer Maria on but inside I was dying. I felt like I'd lost everything and I didn't know where to turn.

One evening I went into the bathroom of the apartment we were all sharing in the little rented apartment and I stared at myself in the mirror. What had become of my life? I'd spent years, decades even, pouring all of my efforts into being Kelly Holmes, being someone.

In hindsight, I know my reasons for hanging my hopes so heavily on Olympic success weren't just about wanting to be a good athlete. It was about proving to myself and to the world that I was worthy, that I was good at something, that I was worth sticking around for. It was about giving myself an identity outside of the sexuality I'd been hiding all those years. It was about making sure I had a life and a career I could be proud of after years in an institution that had chipped away at my self-esteem. Winning was about so much more than a medal.

And now, standing in front of that mirror, I couldn't see a winner. I could see a broken person whose body was giving up on her.

I still don't know what made me do it but I found myself reaching for a pair of nail scissors that were in a glass on the side in the bathroom. I felt the cold metal of them against my skin as I touched them against my left arm and then, after running water from the taps, I pointed the tip against the inside of my bicep and pressed until I saw red. As the blood pooled on my skin, I felt an instant sense of relief.

The pain was nothing compared with the torture of training on my injured leg and if anything it was a distraction. It was like, for a second, all the thoughts swimming around my mind stopped and I had something else to focus on. I was a complete mess and I was having a breakdown. The only way I can describe it is that it was a way to feel something different, to snap me out of the desperate spiral of grief for my career.

To begin with, it was about the injuries and my fear that my athletics career could be over once and for all, so I started making another cut in my arm for every day I'd had to miss training. After that, every day that I couldn't train I would lock myself in the bathroom and do the same thing. Margo and Maria would be chatting and laughing away in the next room, oblivious to the fact I was falling apart behind that locked door. But what started as a breakdown over my physical form quickly opened the floodgates to a much bigger mental crisis.

All my fears and insecurities from the trauma I experienced as a child and in the army started to come to the surface. I found myself obsessing over what I would do if my athletics career came to an end. I couldn't go back to the army now. By then I'd got wind of the supposed changes to army culture following the lifting of the homosexuality ban, but I just didn't believe it was true.

All those same people who tried to sniff out gay men and women, who raided bunks and screamed homophobic slurs in my face were all still there. You couldn't tell me they'd suddenly changed their views on same-sex couples just because of a piece of paper from a court, it takes years for a culture like that to change. So what else was out there for me? Who was I really if I was no longer Sgt Holmes or Olympian Kelly?

My intrusive thoughts soon turned into a full-on identity crisis and up that mountain in France I had no one to turn to. Margo even started to try to keep me away from Maria as she could tell something was wrong and she didn't want my negativity running off on her.

I started to realise that I needed some professional help, because I didn't understand for the life of me what was leading me to hurt myself – weren't my injuries punishment enough? Yet the thought of telling anyone the real reasons behind my breakdown filled me with horror. Sure, I could tell them about the injuries, but how could I make them understand just why the stakes were so high for me without telling them the truth about my past and who I really was? Telling them the truth was out of the question. I knew only too well what the press did when they got hold of even a rumour about my sexuality, so what if I told a medical professional and they tipped them off that it was all true?

Instead I decided to try to deal with my feelings myself. I carried on cutting but did it in such a controlled way, I wouldn't be found out. The last thing I needed was for Margo or Maria to see that weakness as well as my injury so I cut on my arms and on my chest which would be covered by my running vest and t-shirts. I became expert in covering the wounds with little plasters and then, when they healed, pasting make-up over the scars to stop them being noticed.

Over the next couple of weeks, to my surprise, my leg started to get better and I was able to get out of the pool and start running again. There was no time for softly-softly. If I wanted to salvage anything of my last season before the Olympics I had to get stuck straight back in. I did three races in the space of a week in Zurich, Berlin and London and finished fourth, ninth and first. Not perfect but not the disaster it could have been, so when Maria and Margo moved to St Moritz for the last training stop before Paris, I went too.

While I was in St Moritz I went for a sports massage with a specialist and while I was there I plucked up the courage to ask if I could see a local doctor about another private matter. Sitting in the clinic in front of the female doctor, I told her I'd been struggling with my mood. I didn't go into all the details of why or just how low I'd become, because I knew she would assume it was simply linked to my injuries, and that was fine by me.

She told me it was common to have periods of depression when you undergo severe physical and mental stress and said she would ordinarily prescribe me with SSRIs or anti-depressants. But anti-doping was already such a hot topic in the athletics world and you had to be so careful what you put into your body so there was no way I was going to take anything that could be misconstrued and I didn't know if anti-depressants were performance-enhancing, plus I couldn't ask any of my team. Instead the lady recommended some herbal pills made from the cacao plant that she said could help without chemical intervention. It sounded stupid but I was so desperate I was ready to try anything and, as a self-confessed chocoholic, it made sense that it might work.

I'm not sure whether the pills actually helped as I only took two – still worried about what they were – or it was just my improved physical strength that gave me some hope back, but I was soon feeling on slightly steadier ground and decided to go for it in Paris. I just entered the 800m not the 1500m because, with my recent injuries, I thought it would give me a better chance.

Maria was in the same race and by some miracle while she took gold, I took the silver medal. Okay, I didn't beat her but training with Maria had clearly paid off and after the season I'd had I would take second to anyone! On the finish line I was totally overwhelmed with joy and relief and Maria and I hugged each other to congratulate one another. Big mistake.

Jealousy over our joint success and a hungry watching press devoured rumours from other athletes that not only were Maria and I in a relationship but that we'd rigged the race so that we would both get the two top spots. Of course it was total nonsense because there were six other people in the race that could run however they wanted, but this time the rumours hit even harder and I'm really sad to say it spelled the end of my friendship with Maria. She was really upset about the stories. She was a much bigger celebrity back in Mozambique than I was in the UK so she got a really tough time from the media back home.

It got to the point where it was awkward for us to even be seen training together. We just wanted the focus to be on our performances not our personal relationship so, with only one race left in the season, we decided to spend less time together.

The main point of this is not about Maria, it's to highlight that whilst I stood on the rostrum no one knew what was going on with my mental health. I didn't just win a silver medal, I won a psychological battle, no amount of press insinuations could deter from the fact that I had done something pretty remarkable that day. It showed me the power of my mind and that even though I was hurting on the inside, I was still winning.

We all have the power within us to get through the tough times and that's called resilience.

12

If I Ain't Got You

2004: THE YEAR OF THE OLYMPICS IN ATHENS AND my last chance to fulfil my dream. At almost 34, it was now or never. After my third season majorly affected by physical injury and a mental breakdown casting a shadow over the previous year, I could've gone into 2004 feeling pretty hopeless.

The pressures of speculation about my sexuality and accusations of cheating had weighed heavy on me as I recovered from the World Championships but something happened in January of that year that I can't explain.

Out of nowhere, through the shadows of depression, doubt and fear, came a sudden clear and total confidence like I've never known before: I wasn't only going to go to Athens in the summer, I was going to win gold. I can't describe where the feeling came from or why it hit me at that moment. If I was a religious person I might have called it divine intervention but it was such a clear feeling, it was almost a premonition. It wasn't visualisation like I'd practised before to try to get myself in the zone, it was real. I could almost sense that feeling I would have when I crossed the finish line and claimed Olympic glory for the first time.

I even wrote it in my diary to capture that feeling in case it went away. I wrote: 'I have dreamed forever to be the best at what I do. Some dreams have come true, but my biggest ones are still out there and I really want them to become reality. I have gone through a lot to realise my dreams. I have the passion, dedication, willpower and heart to achieve my ultimate goals. I have put my life and soul into this, given up my life to pursue what I know is my destiny. I just pray that for once I can be given the lift to get through this year with no struggles, no injuries and a lighted spirit of guidance. I hope 2004 can bring me more happiness, success, purpose than ever before.'

Now I know I'd had that feeling that it was going to be my year before, and it didn't always end the way I'd hoped, but this time it was last chance saloon. One final roll of the dice, and deep down I knew that all the years of training, physical and mental battles must count for something. Still in the back of my mind somewhere was this feeling that if I won Olympic gold, that would define who I was forever, no one could take it away. I naively thought that if I won, people wouldn't think about my sexuality or who I decided to be with, or try to delve into my mental health issues. I would just be Kelly Holmes, Olympic champion.

Back in Johannesburg, life was pretty lonely at the start of the year as Maria had distanced herself from me after all the rumours, and was now spending lots of time training away. Agnes was going back and forth to Namibia, so instead I decided to pack up and head back to my place in Potchefstroom where there was a community of athletes from all over the world training. I soon found myself in a better place.

In the first few months of that year, I was on fire! I won my 13th British title in the 800m at the indoor AAA meet in Sheffield as well as 1500m in Glasgow and Stockholm. Margo was buzzing every time I spoke to her on the phone or I sent her my times. I was in such good form. My mind seemed to be on an up-curve too and my self-harm was under control most of the time. I would have the odd bad day when things wouldn't go right or when I let myself think about the weight of my hidden sexuality but, for the most part, I was so focused on success I didn't allow myself to dwell on it.

I was reunited with Maria and Jeff in Birmingham where we were both running in a 1000m race ahead of the 1500m event in the World Championships in Budapest in March. I was on cloud nine when I not only won but broke the British and European records. But there was a dark cloud of controversy around the win as Maria had tripped over when she tried to overtake me, and this time there were rumours swirling that I'd tripped her.

Of course I hadn't and even the commentators said she tried to overtake me on the inside where there was clearly no space, but the accusations were hurtful. What was it with the press trying to make drama with our friendship all the time? One minute I was supposedly seeing her and then I was supposedly sabotaging her race. Margo told me to ignore it and let the dust settle, and stay focused on Budapest, so that's what I did, but it was a real insight into the impact rumours can have on your focus and mental health – something I was to learn much more of later that year.

The World Championships were even more dramatic. This time it was my turn to fall, in the 1500m. 500m from the end I decided to make my break for it and try to pass the rest of the field but I tripped and went hurtling to the ground, grazing all down my side and twisting my back. I got back to my feet and completed the race but came in a disappointing ninth position.

Maria and I saw one another for the first time since the tripping scandal as she was there running and I went to cheer her on. I didn't want there to be bad feelings between us so I cheered her round the track. I have to say that for all the nit-picking, in my eyes, she was undoubtedly the best 800m runner in the world, full stop – I was delighted when she took the title yet again. Still, I was gutted about my disaster. I flew home and went to spend a week or two in Kent before going back to South Africa. I just needed to see my friends and my family and they were great as ever, cheering me up and telling me how proud they were of me.

Training in the run-up to the Olympic trials was a lonely journey. I flew out to Oregon, USA, to see Margo. Maria was there too and although it was still slightly awkward, we just got on with training because that was all we were there to do. We all relocated to Madrid along with Jeff ahead of the trials because the climate would be similar to Athens, but it was a bleak time. I was running really erratically since my fall and I no longer had that camaraderie with Maria that made all the training more fun. I sat alone in my tiny bedroom at night, watching DVDs and wishing I was back home with my family and my dogs. Still, in the back of my mind I just kept telling myself: a couple more months and you'll have that medal around your neck.

Even though Dave and I had parted ways and I'd split from Sarah, they were both great during that time. I would text Dave my times and keep him up to date with my progress and message Sarah with funny anecdotes about not being able to speak Spanish and getting stuck trying to communicate in sign language. I felt really supported by them and began to feel more and more distant from Maria and Margo. Understandably, I felt like I was always second fiddle as Margo and Maria had been working together for 13 years. I was still the new girl by comparison. Plus, all the dramas had left a sour atmosphere.

Then came another issue. I was not training with the team anymore but the way I was running, I decided I might want to get selected for both the 1500m and the 800m at the Olympics as I didn't want to ruin my chances of winning a gold by putting all my eggs in one basket. I'd been running great times over the shorter distance, going on to win the 800m at the Olympic trials in Manchester. UK Athletics selected me for both the 800m and the 1500m for Athens as they knew the 1500m was my main focus and I was still number one in Great Britain for that distance.

The problem was that Maria did the 800m as that was her event and she was defending Olympic champion. Margo said she couldn't be in both our Olympic teams if we were going to compete against one another. She told me if I decided to run the 800m, she could not be my coach at the Games.

However, I had already decided that for my mental health, my mindset and for support, I would go with Team GB to the holding camp in Cyprus, where we would do two final weeks of training ahead of the Games. That decision was instrumental in my preparation. I didn't have to make my final decision about which distance I was going for until the last minute so I decided to just focus on my training.

Margo gave me a training schedule which I stuck to religiously and I loved being in Cyprus with the rest of the team. It started to really feel like we were in it together, representing our country, and we wanted to go home with as many medals as possible.

I shared a lovely villa in a new golf resort in Aphrodite Hills with Liz Yelling, a marathon runner, and it was idyllic. The atmosphere in the team was amazing, so relaxed but focused. My team, physio Alison Rose, training partner Tony Whitman and Performance Director Zara Hyde Peters were fantastic and, for the first time, I felt this amazing sense of calm.

Of course it didn't all go without a hitch because I wouldn't be Kelly without a bit of drama. I got bitten by a millipede that I found in my bed – yes, bed! – about a week in and ended up in hospital from the poison. But thankfully the pain passed and didn't affect my running. Insects aside, it was all going to plan.

* * * * *

I'm not a religious person but I've always been a big believer that things happen for a reason and that the universe gives us signs to guide us on our way. I think it all started when I met Lisa in Sainsbury's that day – what were the chances of us bumping into each other like that at that specific time after living down the road all those years? I later realised it had been predicted by a Tarot card reader I'd been to see months before, who told me I was going to meet someone who'd been looking for me. Since then, I have always believed in fate.

The week before I was due to move from Cyprus to Athens for the biggest races of my career, I got two of those signs that have stayed with me until this day. The first was all about my hair. Ever since that summer when I was a kid and Mum took me to the salon to get my massive afro tamed with disastrous results, my hair has been the bane of my life.

My only option back then if I was going to be able to train and run without it getting in the way was to have braids to keep it out of my face. When I went to Cyprus for the Olympics training camp, I decided I would get my braids re-done just before the Games so they would be fresh and tight, ready for my big performance. I guess it was superstition really, but I just wanted everything to be perfect.

Most of the runners up in the mountain villas were in the endurance team but a few sprinters managed to gatecrash our little paradise including Linford Christie, Olympic champion in 1992, Darren Campbell (who went on to win gold in the 4x100m relay in Athens) and Daniel Plummer, his training partner. Daniel told me he could do my hair.

"Honestly, I do my sister's hair back home, it's no problem," he assured me. So I took his word it would all be fine. We agreed he would do it that night.

Later that day, a big group of us went down to the beach after our last big training sessions, for some natural cold therapy (years before it was trendy!). We started messing around and skimming stones when a British woman who was clearly on holiday with her family came over to me and introduced herself as Patricia.

"I never usually do this but just in case you ever need your hair doing, I'm a hairdresser back home in Wembley so you should get in touch."

She left but then came running back down the beach to me and slipped a business card into my hand with her name and phone number on it. What a weird coincidence! I took her card and thought at the time, 'that'll come in handy one day', but I didn't know it would be so soon.

Back at camp that night I sat on a chair with Daniel behind me, afro in full glory, as he tried desperately to part my crazy mane to plait it into braids. The problem was he didn't even have a proper comb and a pen lid wasn't cutting it. Long story short, it was a disaster.

I told him not to worry as I remembered Patricia's card. Could I call her in the middle of her nice relaxing holiday and ask for her help? I was desperate and she had offered. Plus, if I won, I guess she could tell people she was a hairdresser to an Olympic champion! I called her a couple of times before she answered and then when she did, I felt sheepish.

"I'm really sorry but I'm in a bit of a mess and I could really do with your help," I told her.

Patricia turned out to be one of the nicest people I've ever met and I'm convinced she was put on the beach that day just for me. She came over the next day with her daughter Stacia and calmed me down completely, and then did the most amazing job braiding my hair. I felt mentally and physically ready to take on the world, like you do when you have a new hairdo. More importantly, it would be one less thing to think or worry about.

I told her she was a life-saver and I would be back in touch when I got home after the Games. I think she probably thought I was just saying that, but I wasn't. When I finally got back I looked her up and she ended up doing my hair for years and becoming a great friend.

The other sign that week came in the form of one of my absolute idols. Ever since I was a teenager I've absolutely loved Tina Turner. I loved her music, of course, that amazing raspy voice and the don't-give-a-shit attitude, but I also loved everything she stood for.

To me she was the ultimate survivor, after a really tough life and an abusive marriage to being a global superstar, she was so powerful and resilient. In her later years when she moved to Switzerland to be with her new husband she became spiritual, practising Buddhism, yoga and meditation, something that's brought me so much peace in the past few years too.

In Cyprus I was in the back of the car on the way to the track for my last session with Tony and Zara. The countdown was on and I knew I only had 24 hours to make my decision about whether or not I was going to enter the 800m, the 1500m or both, so my mind was racing. I'd been running great 800m times but did I want to lose Margo from my team at the last minute?

Cypriot songs were playing on the radio as I tried to mentally prepare and I was beginning to feel so anxious when I literally said: "I could really do with listening to Tina Turner *The Best* right now". Literally as I spoke, the song came on! I heard that unmistakable: "*Dun... dun, dun... dun...*" come from the speakers. Unbelievable. It was the intro to *The Best* – Tina had come to help me! Tony cranked up the volume and I sang along to the lyrics at the top of my voice.

> *Give me a lifetime of promises and a world of dreams,*
> *Speak a language of love like you know what it means,*
> *It can't be wrong,*
> *Take my heart and make it strong, baby.*
> *You're simply the best,*
> *Better than all the rest,*
> *Better than anyone,*
> *Anyone I've ever met.*

I defy anyone to listen to that track and not feel a massive confidence boost. I know it was meant to be a romantic song but I think, like me, people associate it with strength and achievement. It meant so many things to me too. It was like she was singing to me, telling me I could do whatever I set my heart on and that I was strong enough to do whatever felt right. Everything was going to be okay.

I was so fired up I had the best training session and ran some of my fastest times ever, I felt like I was floating on air. By the end of the day I'd made my decision. I knew I had a chance of a medal in the 800m, so I made the biggest decision of my life – to double up! I texted Dave my times from that day. He had now become a mentor and still my greatest supporter and he messaged back: 'You have to go for it'.

When I called Margo I was nervous about what she was going to say but I'd never been more clear I was making the decision that was right for me. I was pleasantly surprised when Margo said I had to do whatever I thought was best for me and that even though she couldn't be on my team, she would support me in whatever I decided to do. She told me to follow my heart, and that's what I did. Later that night I wrote a press release revealing my intention to run in both the 800m and the 1500m. In for a penny, in for a pound as they say.

I still think it was fate I heard Tina that day and she's remained an idol of mine and a huge inspiration throughout my life. For my 53rd birthday (which I called 39+14 of course!) I went to see the West End show for the second time, with some of my new friends. I absolutely love it. Everyone was up in the stalls singing and dancing along to *Proud Mary* and there was a huge standing ovation at the end. It really showed how loved Tina was and how much she meant to so many people.

When her death was reported earlier this year in 2023, I was really sad but also happy for her that she died peacefully in a place she loved, after living a quiet life of meditation by the lake and in a relationship with the person she loved, out of the way of the prying eyes and judgement of the media or anyone else who had tried to hurt her in the past. I think that's a decent way to end your days on this planet. I have since seen the show for a third time, there was something even more powerful about it after Tina's passing and the fact that I have become friends with Elesha, who currently plays her in the musical, seems another twist of fate!

* * * * *

Being a woman who has spent her entire life trying not to attract too much attention or give anyone reason to probe into her private life, the last thing I needed when I was about to run the most important races of my life was to be at the centre of a media storm. So, when we arrived at the Olympic Village outside Athens ahead of the Games, I was relieved that the descending British press already had one golden girl on their minds – Paula Radcliffe.

Paula was an amazing 10,000m athlete and one of our greatest Marathon runners. I had known her for years, we got on really well and she was touted as Team GB's big hope for gold medals in the endurance races in Athens. Her form was great and she had a consistent record whereas I had a reputation for getting injured or suffering terrible luck just when it mattered. I think everyone knew me as a reliable medallist having won 11 major medals already, but some people were nervous that it wouldn't be third time lucky for me at the Olympics as I'd hoped.

Thankfully for me, because of all the hype around Paula I was able to escape most of the attention and focus on settling into my accommodation. The room was small but comfortable and I pinned up all the good luck cards and notes from my friends and family on the wardrobe. They weren't going to be there to see me race as it was too expensive to travel but I knew they would be thinking of me and again I didn't want the distraction of them being there while I was getting in the zone.

I did one interview with the BBC about why I'd decided to do the 800m as well as the 1500m at the last minute, but I only spoke in broad terms about my ambitions. I didn't want to give too much away about my form in case I jinxed it and I didn't ever talk to the press about my personal life in case they thought that gave them free rein to delve into it and find something I didn't want them to find.

An Olympic village is like something you never experience unless you make an Olympic team and it's an amazing atmosphere. Nations from all over the world come together, sharing the massive food halls, gyms and social spaces, wearing their national team kit and flying their flags with pride. The night before my first heat I laid my kit out on the chair, something that became a ritual throughout my career, and went to sleep early with my headphones in, listening to Alicia Keys, *If I Ain't Got You*, which became my anthem for the Games.

Some people want it all,
But I don't want nothing at all,
If it ain't you, baby,
If I ain't got you, baby,
Some people want diamond rings,
Some just want everything,
But everything means nothing,
If I ain't got you, yeah!

I set off to the stadium early the next morning armed with energy drinks, a ham and cheese roll and my lucky charm, a silver dog tag engraved with the British flag. I kissed it before every race and always made sure to look for the British flag in the stadium the second I emerged from the tunnel onto the track. It was a reminder of the pride and honour I felt in representing my country on the biggest sporting stage in the world. It was a similar feeling to the pride of serving the Crown and my country during my army years and it meant a huge amount to me and still does now.

I cruised through my first heat and won without too much trouble. The semi-final went according to plan too, so I just had to keep my cool on my rest day before the final. During that time we had triumph and disaster in the camp. Hepthathlete Kelly Sotherton came home with a bronze in her first ever Olympics and was elated. I was so pleased for her.

We stayed up talking until 2am because I couldn't sleep, and she was coming down from the huge adrenaline rush. I knew exactly how that felt after my bronze in Sydney. But I also knew what Paula was feeling when she had to pull up in the marathon because of an injury, in what should have been the biggest race of her life. The same happened later in the 10,000m. It was heartbreaking to watch her as she came off the track. I prayed that it wouldn't happen to me again this year.

The night before the final I had another 'sign'. As I was listening to Alicia again on my bed, a massive gust of wind swirled around my neck and I found myself jumping up shouting, "I'm going to do it!". It was the most bizarre moment.

On the day of the 800m final, I was surprisingly calm. When I reached the warm-up track, Margo came over, winked at me and said "good luck", patting me on the back. Maria ran past and touched my hand on the start line and said the same thing. I knew that it was each woman for herself, there were no hard feelings there. Then my mind cleared completely as I lined up in lane three of the track. The gun sounded and, just like in training, I executed each of my tactics; no trips, no falls, no sudden bursts of pain – it was all going just as it should. Ten metres before the end of the track, as I was neck and neck with Maria, I told myself to relax, dropped my shoulders and, in a split second, I was crossing the finish line.

FIRST! Surely not? That couldn't have happened.

I looked up at the big screen and saw the replay, and it was true. I was first, I'd won gold. I was totally overwhelmed.

The iconic picture that everyone remembers of me crossing the finish line – where my eyes are popping out of my head in utter disbelief – still has people cheering when I do my public speaking, and I still well up at the memory. I was on top of the world.

Then, time passes in a blur of press conferences and photographers and doping control before you finally stand on the rostrum and accept your medal. I remember thinking that nothing has ever compared to this; remember this moment, as the Union Jack was raised and *God Save The Queen* rang out around the stadium.

Back at the Village, I would have loved to celebrate but the 1500m heats started the next day so I didn't have much time to recover. The weird feeling was that despite winning gold in the 800m, it was the 1500m that I had dreamed of winning since I was 14. But my family had other ideas... Back home, Mum, Dad, Kevin, Stuart, Lisa, Penny, Danny, along with all my mates (and as I later found out nearly the whole of Great Britain) were partying the night away over my win. They couldn't believe it and kept on calling me to tell me how proud they were of me – each time getting louder and more animated. Although it was lovely to hear them so happy and proud of me, I had to tell them to go and to let me sleep. I had another race to get ready for. I put my medal under the pillow and drifted off.

At the stadium the next day, everyone wanted to talk to me and congratulate me, the press interest was insane. There were photographers and reporters everywhere asking for interviews but I stuck to my usual plan of keeping my head down, only giving one short BBC interview about my win.

Little did I know, the press were going crazy about that. I was their new focus. The team kept it all away from me, but I found out later that I was on the back and middle pages of most of the newspapers and even on the front of some too. I was the new golden girl and now I'd won one, they were rooting for me to bring home another. I'm really glad I didn't know just how mad things were back home because it would have been a huge distraction.

Back at the track that night, I followed exactly the same warm-up routine as I had for the 800m and just tried to remain calm and focused. This time Margo was able to talk to me properly because Maria wasn't running in the 1500m, but she didn't have any changes to my tactics and so I decided to go out there and do what I'd waited a lifetime to do.

Once again, I got through my heat without too much trouble, although I wasn't as fresh as I'd been for the 800m. Sally Gunnell – our 1992 Olympic champion – became part of my post-race ritual. Whether she was interviewing me or not, she was there as I crossed the line to hand me the cashew nuts I'd given her at the beginning of the competition. In the semi the next day, I felt confident and Margo had told me to just do what I needed to get through but not show the opposition my full hand, so I ran a steady race then towards the end hung back and finished second.

There was one more rest day before the final and that was the toughest one. It was a mental challenge to try to psych myself up as if it was my first race of the Games and I hadn't already won a medal. I wanted to feel the same sense of 'now or never' I would be feeling as if I was going for gold for the first time. So I hid my medal and tried to pretend it didn't exist.

On the day of the final, as I lined up for what I knew would probably be my last ever Olympic race, it felt completely different. This time British fans were shouting my name and cheering me as my name was called. Rather than just announcing me as Kelly Holmes, this time the tannoy boomed, "800m Olympic champion Kelly Holmes". I had to block it all out and just concentrate on the race in hand. This was my race, and the gold was the one I'd come to Athens for in the first place.

When the starting gun sounded, it was as though no one else was in the stadium except me and the other runners. I hung back to begin with just as I'd planned and had executed in every other race. On the final lap, another bizarre experience happened. On the back straight with about 250m to go, I felt as though something was lifting me up by my shoulders as I passed other runners in the field. I was floating as though I had wings. I could feel my legs moving but I couldn't feel my feet pounding the track, it was like I was running on air. I was exhausted but the adrenaline was pumping through my veins. About 120m from the finish line, I knew I needed to make a break. I remember looking around to see where the danger may be coming from then, about 50m from the end, I can't even describe it but it felt like something swept me up and lifted me right over the finish line. I was in first place again.

Suddenly reality dawned and I crumbled to my knees, exhausted as the roar of the crowd filled my ears. I had tears in my eyes as the delirium faded and I realised I'd fulfilled my entire life's dream not once but twice. I thought nothing could match the feeling of winning one gold but I can tell you now – doing the double was something else.

The same blur followed, my victory lap, flashing camera bulbs and screaming fans followed by an interview with Sally where I can't even remember what I said. Then it was back to the rostrum for the second time and as I bowed my neck for my hero, Lord Seb Coe to place the medal around my neck, I felt invincible.

Back at the village that night I wanted to go out and celebrate with the rest of the British team, so a few of us tried to get a taxi into town. But it was before the days of Uber and we had no local taxi numbers so after spending some time sitting on a kerb waiting, we gave up and went back into the village to the 24-hour canteen with rower Matthew Pinsent, who was also celebrating his gold medal, and we raided the freezer for ice creams. Not how I envisaged the best night of my life, but it felt incredible.

What I didn't know was that the double gold had truly cemented me in the history books as being the first woman in Great Britain to win two gold medals at the same Olympic Games.

13

National Treasure

AFTER A WHIRLWIND OF EMOTIONS AND TWO historic victories at the Olympics, coming home to Great Britain was a moment I'd waited for all my life. I was returning glorious, with not one but two gold medals around my neck – it was a total dream come true for me, but I never really stopped to think about what it would mean.

I knew there was a buzz about how well I'd done because Mum told me on the phone that I was on the front page of all the national newspapers after my second win. I still have those papers to this day, with that picture of me crossing the finishing line and the one of me draped in a British flag. A couple of them are framed on the wall in my little memorabilia room at the top of my house because they made me proud, of course, but also because they reminded me of what I'd done – I still couldn't believe it!

What I didn't realise was that my wins also made me public property.

As the plane touched down on British soil, I could already feel the anticipation building. Being a medal winner, British Airways had put me and the other Team GB medallists in Business Class, which is always a great perk; I will never turn that one down!

As we landed on the runway, I was asked to lead the team off the plane and as the doors opened we could see a huge crowd of press, officials and BA staff awaiting us. After taking a photo on the steps, we made our way to the arrivals. All the medallists were escorted to a press conference before being reunited with loved ones. But I was not expecting what followed.

Having competed in two previous Olympic Games before, I knew the reception that normally awaits the British teams as we arrive back to the UK. It doesn't matter what sport you compete in or if you medalled or not, the families, friends and fans of the athletes always come out to greet and congratulate you. But the reception that awaited this time was beyond anything I could have imagined.

The hall was packed! People screaming with excitement, cheering fans waving flags and holding banners adorned with messages of congratulations and the press hustling for photos as my mum came over to hug me, crying with pride. As I was reunited with my family it started to dawn on me just how big my wins had been over here.

My dad, Kevin, Stuart, Penny, Lisa and Danny were all there to greet me, it was incredibly overwhelming. There was this big limo waiting to take us all back to Hildenborough, a journey that was a blur of excitement and emotion. What I didn't know was that my wider family and friends had organised a surprise party for me at a local pub called the Hilden Manor where Neil the owner, Claire and Emma my sister-in-law were helping get it all ready. As I walked through the door, the roar of excitement and celebration hit me.

By now I was so exhausted, but the adrenaline of it all carried me through. It was so lovely to share this incredible moment with so many people I loved. The sense of pride and joy was palpable, and I couldn't help but be moved by the genuine warmth and affection shown by everyone, they were so proud of me.

Returning to Mum's house was crazy. She had put red, white and blue flags up outside the house and I saw tents on the grass in front of a hedge. When we got inside and sat down, she drew the curtains.

"What you doing?" I asked.

"It's the paparazzi," she told me. "They're in those tents opposite, they've been there all week waiting for you to come home."

It just felt so strange. It's one thing having my photo taken by a mob of photographers inside the stadium in Athens after my wins, then at the airport with the team, but how did they find out where my mum lived? And why were they there? What were they looking out for? I just didn't get it or the media intrusion as I had never had it before, it felt uneasy.

It made me start to think about the pictures that had gone around the world of me crossing the finish line and standing on the rostrum. Now the entire world knew who I was – or they thought they did. Already in the midst of all the celebrations I had a nervous feeling. The Kelly Holmes who had become a sporting legend and had been beamed around the world into people's living rooms on their TV screens, was still just Kelly from a small village in Kent, a retired soldier who'd made history by going on to win two gold medals.

The real Kelly, who had been hounded and raided in the army over rumours of her sexuality and who was terrified of coming out, was someone completely different. The only thing they would find out about my personal life if they looked back in the newspapers would be a relationship with a man – Jason – which was actually just a friendship. It makes me unhappy to think that's what was going through my mind back then, but at the time I couldn't let those demons ruin what I knew should be the best week of my life so I brushed them to the back of my mind.

The highlight of my homecoming was definitely the parade organised in my honour by Tonbridge and Malling Borough Council a couple of days later. A huge yellow open-top bus was arranged to pick me up outside the scout hut on Riding Lane in Hildenborough, just round the corner from Mum's house, ready to drive me to Tonbridge on a parade route. All my family came on the bus with me as well as Dave, Miss Page, my PE Teacher and, of course, Kerrie. The local newspaper sent a reporter and a photographer. I wore my medals and had a Union flag draped around me as we set off. The atmosphere was incredible.

We'd been told to expect about 40,000 people but it ended up being double that, can you imagine? Unbelievable. Travelling through the streets I used to pedal through on my bike, now I was on top of the bus, being greeted by a sea of smiling faces, waving flags, and cheering at the top of their lungs and chanting my name.

The energy and enthusiasm were infectious, and I couldn't help but be swept up in the sheer joy of the moment. The streets were lined with people of all ages, eagerly awaiting my arrival. Some of them knew me all my life and others were just proud and excited that someone from our little corner of the world had achieved something so amazing. The cheers and applause echoed through the air, creating an atmosphere of celebration and pride. It was a moment that I will always cherish, as I realised the impact my achievements had on the whole nation and especially my home town.

As I waved to the crowd, I couldn't help but reflect on the journey that had led me to this point. The countless hours of training, the sacrifices made, and the unwavering support of my family, friends, and coaches had all culminated in this incredible moment.

It was a testament to the power of perseverance, determination, and the unwavering self-belief. Throughout the parade, I made sure to take in every moment, to lock eyes with the fans who had stood by me throughout my career. Their support had been the driving force behind my success, and I wanted to express my gratitude personally. The smiles, tears, and heartfelt messages of congratulations from the crowd filled my heart.

But the niggling feeling in the back of my mind came back when the press photographer kept snapping me on top of the bus, taking thousands of pictures which I knew would be all over the papers the next day. What if one of the 80,000 people in the crowd or someone looking at the picture in the papers the next day recognised me from one of my rare trips to a gay bar in Slough in my Aldershot heyday, or knew someone who'd had a fling with me in the army? People could make a lot of money selling stories about me to the newspapers and then everyone would know my big secret.

As I looked out into the crowds, I felt myself start to shake with the same fear I'd felt back at Beaconsfield as I waited for the RMP to raid my bunk, terrified they'd find evidence of me being gay. I grabbed the camera from the photographer and said I thought I should take some photos, just so the attention was off me for a second. But of course it wasn't, was it!

The homecoming celebrations continued long into the night. The speeches, the laughter, and people sharing stories of inspiration were a reminder of the impact my achievements had on others. Everyone was desperate for an interview with someone close to me, especially as there wasn't much known about me and that's how I wanted it to stay. Thankfully my family and friends never dreamt of speaking to the press behind my back, and, in fact, the only person who did sell a story didn't know I was gay because he hadn't seen me for nearly two decades – 'sperm donor' Derrick. Clearly the money offers were too enticing for him and he gave an interview telling the newspaper that he taught me everything I knew, posing for a photo with a pair of trainers around his neck.

However, I couldn't shake the feeling that I felt more exposed now I was back on home ground. Would anyone want to destroy me and try to out me? In the LGBT community, as it was known then, the worst thing you could do was out someone, and the worst thing that could happen to you was to be outed!

What you have to remember is that society can be so cruel, people's opinions about the way you live your life can be damaging to your soul. Many people from all walks of life have been vilified for just being themselves. They have been hounded, bullied, mistreated and targeted to the point that some sadly have taken their own lives, all because they live life in a way that doesn't suit others' preconception of what 'normal' is. It's normal for me to be attracted to women. I can't help how I feel or what I am. But the fear of being outed, and with my irrational fear of being potentially reprimanded by the military in some way, was enough to always dampen my spirits even while I was on top of the world.

It was the start of a spiral of self-doubt and fear that stayed with me for the next 18 years.

* * * * *

One thing us Brits do well is national pride. In the weeks after I returned home from Athens, the phone didn't stop ringing with people inviting me to showbiz parties, media appearances and awards ceremonies. I was hot property and everyone wanted a piece of the woman who had won two Olympic gold medals after 20 years of trying; the first British woman to win two individual gold medals at the same Games. Only achieved by one other person, Albert Hill, in 1920. I think, as a nation, we also love an underdog so to see me live my dream after so many injuries and setbacks was the perfect fairytale ending that everyone loved – especially the press.

For me, though, it felt totally overwhelming. I had been in the press before and had an element of media attention when they twisted my friendship with Maria and on another occasion after they thought I had accused an athlete, Yolanda Cheplak, of cheating back in 2002 (that wasn't true), but now the interest was on a whole new level. Plus, so far they'd never actually got hold of any real information about my past or my private life and I wanted to keep it that way.

I started turning down a lot of the engagements I was offered, although there were some I just couldn't miss because I knew they would be once-in-a-lifetime experiences. The first week I was back, the call came from the Michael Parkinson Show, asking me to be a guest that Friday night. Parky was huge back then and I remember watching all the big Hollywood stars when

I was growing up. I couldn't turn that down. What if someone amazing was on with me and I missed it? I said yes, but there was one problem. All of my clothes were back in South Africa and all I'd brought with me to Athens was one pair of jeans, a pair of combat trousers and a load of sports gear. I told the producer I had nothing to wear and she asked me what kind of thing I would like, saying that the wardrobe department would be able to sort me out. I told her I wanted something black and preferably not a dress.

Sure enough, when I arrived to have my make-up done at the TV studios, they had an outfit for me. Black bootcut trousers, a sleeveless black fitted top and black boots. With my hair still in Patricia's cornrows – I had no idea what to do with it with two medals around my neck – I waited nervously backstage. I was the last on and the other two guests were Billy Connolly and Tom Cruise! I couldn't believe I was going to be sharing a stage with such showbiz royalty. When Michael introduced me, I took a deep breath.

"Kelly Holmes is only the third woman in Olympic history to win a double gold medal," he announced. "She's a national treasure and a hero. Ladies and gentlemen, our very own Kelly Holmes!"

Then, to my total surprise as I walked out under the lights, the entire audience was up on their feet giving me a standing ovation, even bigger than the superstars got. Even Tom Cruise was up on his feet and clapping and he greeted me with a big kiss on either cheek before I sat down.

The first thing Parky said to me was: "You must be living the dream." I replied that I was and it was just surreal and overwhelming but, in the back of my mind, I was wondering what else he was going to ask. Looking back at that footage, I look like a rabbit caught in headlights. I'm all in black, speaking quietly and politely and I just don't look 'free'.

The thing that makes me sad is that I said in response to one question about the press attention: "I'm expecting people to come out of the woodwork who don't even know me." I tried to make a joke out of it and deflect the attention by adding "... but Tom knows a lot about that!" which made people laugh. But deep down I think I was maybe giving a warning to anyone who was considering calling the press about my relationships in the army and telling them I was ready to deny anything they tried to say about my sexuality. I wish I'd just been able to enjoy the moment and soak up the atmosphere but clearly those fears were already starting to dominate.

What does make me laugh is that towards the end of the interview, Parky made some comment about me and Tom flirting and asked if he and Bill should leave the two of us to it. If only he'd known. I was probably one of the few women in the room who wasn't swooning over him. Tom was a really lovely man, though, and when I got home I got the shock of my life because he'd called and left a message with Mum asking me to go with him to the premiere of his new film *Collateral* in Leicester Square the following week. I was totally flattered but I turned it down. Yes, I TURNED IT DOWN. Oh my God, how bloody stupid?!

In my defence, not only did I have nothing to wear on a red carpet but I thought if I started rumours about me and anyone in the public eye it would be even more carte blanche for the press to go digging around in my past relationships. Plus, big showbiz events and parties were definitely not my thing.

I never went out socialising. I was happy having a Chinese from the local takeaway with Mum and catching up on the

English telly I'd missed during the five months I'd been away training. But it did make me laugh a month later though when I found out there had been an article in *Sports Illustrated* in the US saying I was dating Tom. What a surreal experience.

The rest of the year flew by in a blur of media appearances and training as I still had to finish my season. In between races I was on a string of TV shows, even filming a guest appearance in the *EastEnders* Christmas special. Then there was GMTV, Des & Mel, and another cameo in *The Kumars at No. 42*. I liked doing the funny ones more than the serious interviews because I was less likely to get asked any awkward questions.

Even after winning two gold medals, I still had more races to run. I officially became world number one in the 1500m at the World Athletics Final in Monaco and the last race of the season was the Newcastle Road Mile, the shorter race held the day before the Great North Run. I was delighted when I broke the course record – what a way to end an amazing season.

In October, the official Olympic Parade through London took place and once again there was a sea of people. This time, the whole of Team GB including the Paralympians were there, so the attention wasn't focused just on me and I was a little more relaxed. The media interest didn't seem to be dying down, though. And with the interest of course came some people out of the woodwork, just like I knew they would.

Most of them I had known briefly in my past, who were wanting to wish me well on my success and new-found popularity. Others were more sinister, with threats to reveal details about my past or my private life. I just ignored them. I wasn't about to allow myself to be blackmailed so I had to just keep calm and try to carry on. That period of my life definitely reminded me of how lucky I was to have the tight-knit group of friends and family that knew me and loved me as I was. They were the ones who kept me sane. Kerrie, Lara and Kim as well as my siblings and Sarah and her family were all really supportive and kept my feet on the ground, being there for me when I needed someone to calm me down and deflect from all the stress of my new-found fame and the anxiety harbouring the truth about my personal life.

One of the best things to happen that year after my wins was when I was announced as the BBC Sports Personality Of The Year. The award was such a prestigious accolade and one that I'd seen lots of great names win in the past so to even be nominated was incredible. Ahead of the awards ceremony I had no idea who had won because it was a public vote announced on the night. Somehow it meant so much more that it was voted for by the British public because the people-pleaser in me that craved acceptance wanted nothing more than to know I was loved by the people I'd been representing in the Olympics.

I was never really a dress person, hence my outfit on Parky, but for this event, fashion designer Scott Henshall offered to make me a bespoke number for the occasion so I accepted. I was nervous at first when I saw the designs because it was short and had big cut-out sections around my midriff, which was far more revealing than anything I would usually wear. At least it was black – my comfort colour!

When Scott arrived at the hotel and I put it on, I loved it. Getting ready for the evening was a mammoth task with a full-on glam squad in my hotel room, it was like nothing I'd experienced before. You don't get dressed up much in the army or on the track! I called Patricia and asked her to come over from Wembley to do my hair. This time, she took out the braids and straightened it into a flicky bob, and a man from the jewellery shop Boodles showed up with diamonds for me to wear. I was never the kind of little girl who dreamt of being a princess, but if I had been, it would have been a dream come true.

On the night of the ceremony, I was so nervous as we awaited the results. Mum, Dad, Kevin and Stuart were all there to support me but they had to sit separately in the audience, while I was next to Steve Cram and Natasha Kaplinsky. They showed a little video about each of the contenders for the award and mine had a string of former British female Olympic gold medallists in it, all sending their messages of luck and support. There was Ann Packer, who won the 800m, Dame Mary Peters, who took the title for the heptathlon and Sally Gunnell, the 400m hurdles champion who I knew so well.

Hearing them all speak about me was so emotional. They were my heroes and they were saying how incredible my achievements were. I wondered whether there would be some young girls sitting at home watching and thinking one day they could join that line-up of incredible sporting women, just like I had.

When they finally announced I'd won I was so choked up I could hardly speak. It meant the world to me to be loved and accepted by the British public. I had my medals, and their approval, and all my family in the audience to enjoy the moment. That was one moment of pure joy in the spotlight that nothing could ruin for me. My life's dreams were complete.

14

Holmes Truths

WHEN I WAS A CHILD, I NEVER GOT TO SPEND MUCH time on my own with Mum. Even though it was just us two for the first four years of my life, being in and out of care and moving around meant I never really had those memories of it being just us at home together. When I moved out to live with Kerrie and her family as a teenager, I'd gone straight from there to basic training, so moving back in with her after Athens was really weird but lovely.

Getting to know your parents as adults can be a strange experience because you appreciate things in them that you never really saw when you were a child or the roles are reversed and you become the parent.

Mum was really loving and caring because she was so proud of me, but she was also so, so nosy. That was one of the things that always made me laugh about her. She couldn't go to the shops or the doctor's surgery or walk the dog without coming back with a story about who was divorcing who or who was moving house or which shops were shutting down. I loved being back in our little village in Kent where everyone knew each other and hearing all her gossip but since the press attention around my wins, the one thing that was tricky was how exposed Mum's house was.

I never quite got over the paps in the bushes and camping in the tents outside when I returned from Athens and we were still getting reporters knocking on the door or waiting for me when I went out for a run, so I knew I needed to get somewhere with a bit more privacy.

"You'll never guess who's splitting up," Mum said when she got back from one of her trips one day. I laughed and rolled my eyes but she told me it was a woman who lived with her husband in a lovely big house at the other end of Hildenborough.

"It'd be perfect for you, Kel," she said. "You should ask her if you can go and have a look."

"I can't do that. It's not even on the market she'll think I'm mad," I said.

But when Mum had an idea in her head she wasn't one to let it go, so off she went to knock on the door herself. I was mortified when she came back to tell me all about it. Mum told the lady she thought I would be interested in putting in an offer and she was delighted, so I went round to see it myself. It had a long private drive and was surrounded by lots of land. It was far more private than Mount Pleasant. The decor inside wasn't exactly to my taste but I could renovate it. And it was close to Mum. I had Dad just up the road too, and the rest of my family all still lived a stone's throw away in Kent.

I put in an offer and it was accepted, so that was that. I was on the move. I couldn't quite believe that, as a kid from a council estate, I now had my own huge place with plenty of land, out-buildings, five bedrooms, a cinema and a massive barn I planned to turn into my gym.

I was looking forward to having a permanent home in England because I wasn't going to need my place in Potchefstroom any longer now I didn't need to train there. I would go back over for holidays, buying an apartment in Stellenbosch, but I'd spent the last 16 years living away a lot either in different barracks or abroad and living out of a suitcase, so I was ready for some home time.

Then one day, fate intervened again. I was out on one of my runs when I passed some farmland. There were three little woolly heads poking out through the fence of one of the fields. I stopped to look at the funny little creatures, not much bigger than lambs but with long necks and curly afros like me when I was a kid. The farmer was in the field with them and I asked what they were.

"They're alpacas," he told me. "Not to be confused with llamas!"

"What do they do?" I asked.

"Well, they run around, eat grass and hedges, that's about it," he replied.

"Will they graze down the field at the back of my house?" I asked, having a brainwave.

He told me that if I wanted to have them I would have to get a few because they're pack animals, but he agreed that they should keep my grass down throughout the year. Plus, they were really cute and I'd already fallen a little bit in love. I agreed to buy two to begin with and they came to live in the field.

At first, it didn't seem like the plan would work. After a few weeks, they were so shy that they just stayed in one little corner of the paddock, eating grass in a little circle. So much for my plans of them keeping the lawn down. So I decided to get another four. Needless to say they didn't become the miracle gardening team I'd hoped for but they did quickly become a big part of my life. I love going out first thing in the morning to feed and talk to them, and giving them a shower with the hosepipe.

One cool thing about being a successful athlete is that you get free stuff. It's usually trainers or sports brands offering to sponsor your running gear. But the coolest thing I was offered came in the same year I got The Boys (as I christened them). A local garden centre wanted to gift me a ride-on mower, just like the one at the big house Mum cleaned when I was a kid. I couldn't believe it and I jumped at the chance. It's funny how things turn out.

When I wrote my first autobiography *Black, White and Gold*, Mum didn't like answering my questions about her past and I didn't like answering hers about my future. She was so desperate for me to be happy. She'd been devastated when she read about my breakdown in France before the Paris championships. She knew I was suffering from injuries but she had no idea just how bad my mental state had become and I think somehow she blamed herself for not knowing, or for not being there.

That's one of the big issues with the stigma surrounding mental health problems like depression and anxiety. Society still looks for someone to blame rather than treating it like a physical illness that has a root cause that needs treating. You wouldn't blame yourself if someone broke their leg but somehow it's harder for friends and family of someone suffering poor mental health to understand.

One thing Mum was definitely right about was that bottling up my fears over coming out was doing me long term damage and no matter what else happened in my life, I would never be truly happy until I was free to just be myself. One of my regrets is that Mum died without ever seeing me as free as I am now but in a way I'm glad that she didn't know the depths of the darkest times I had to go through to get here.

What I now know is that throughout all those conversations we had, I was probably suffering from the delayed trauma of my treatment in the army and so I never told her the full extent of the fear and persecution I suffered back then. It's only been since she died that I've addressed myself just how tough it was to be a gay woman in that institution.

Even though she didn't live to see it, I think Mother Dear would be proud to see how I am now.

* * * * *

No matter how much success I have had in my life, I've never forgotten where I came from or how much I had to fight to get where I am. After Athens, once I was back home where I'd come from, that was clearer in my mind than ever. Most people know me for my Olympic success and now for being on *Loose Women* but a huge part of my life after the Olympics was dedicated to helping other kids like me achieve their potential. That's something that makes me extremely proud.

I always believe one person can make a difference to someone's life like Miss Page and Dave did for me, so it has always been part of me to give back or inspire others and it's still one of the most important things in my life today.

What a lot of people didn't know is that in March 2004, before the Olympics that changed my life forever, I'd already started setting up a scheme for talented young British female runners. I really felt like sport had saved me from some pretty dark times as well as bringing me so much joy and pride, so I wanted other talented young people to have a chance to feel that too. That was when I came up with the idea for 'On Camp With Kelly,' a mentoring and education programme aimed at nurturing and supporting young female athletes on their own journeys to success.

The plan was to provide guidance, inspiration, and practical advice to the next generation. Given my long career, with all its highs and lows, I thought I would be the perfect person to teach them what it took to be a world-class athlete. I hoped then they might go on to achieve great things like I had. What a legacy that would be!

After selecting the first group of girls for the programme early in 2004, I promised I would take them to my training camp in South Africa later that year, barely even registering that I had an Olympic Games to get selected for and hopefully win a gold medal at! That's me all over – always doing 10 things at once and trying to be the best at them all. I never could have imagined how my wins would change my life either. I just assumed I'd be able to fit it all in.

The programme I devised for the selected girls would bring together a team of experienced coaches, sports scientists, and nutritionists to help them reach their potential. I would just be their mentor passing on my years of experiences at the top level of sport and they would hopefully go on to achieve their own goals one day. The idea was that we would work closely with the selected young athletes' coaches and give them everything they needed to get on the road to competing internationally once they left camp and returned to their lives in the UK. But in order to make my vision become a reality, first I needed some cash.

Athletics is amazing, but back then it didn't make you rich.

A lot of the money I had back then was from a bit of sponsorship and my savings from the army. There was no social media for brand collaborations or anything like that back then. There was no cash for posting about protein shakes or sportswear – Facebook only started in February 2004 just before my victories.

Instead, I had to find my own funding. Norwich Union – now Aviva – were the sponsors of British Athletics at the time and so I decided to go and tell them my idea. Even though the Olympics were still to come, I was already a multiple medallist for the Great Britain team so I was well established and mature. I don't know where I got the guts from but I marched into a boardroom with a load of money men and just told them what I wanted. I even asked for my own office in their London building to run the scheme.

Amazingly they were impressed enough to back me and said they would stump up £35,000 to cover the flights, training and insurance for all the young women I picked. And they found me a box room that I lovingly turned into a workspace.

Some people thought I was mad but while I was training for the biggest Olympic Games of my life, I also started the selection process for the first cohort of OCWK participants. I'd been keeping a close eye on regional and national youth events and had already earmarked some great talent. Then we got them all together for a selection process and picked the eight with the most potential. When I went off to Athens, they were already dreaming of my camp in South Africa later that year.

After returning glorious from the Olympics and the world at my feet, everyone questioned why I was still going to take eight giggling girls aged 15-17 halfway across the world. I was at my prime of getting pretty much whatever I wanted, riding high on my success. Appearing at events and having opportunities thrown at me left, right and centre was exciting but I had to stick by my word and give those girls the opportunity I had promised them. I knew what it was like to be let down and I wasn't going to make anyone feel that way.

I decided to take them all out to Potchefstroom for a whole month and give them access to the incredible training facilities, working and training with me. By then I had my five-bedroom house over there and I opened it up to the girls. Two of the female coaches I got on board stayed there with them whilst I moved out for the month to my friend's house.

They loved the whole adventure and I found it so exhilarating seeing these young girls with so much potential, imagining what they could go on to do in the future. The thought of being a part of that gave me far more satisfaction than any of the showbiz parties or events I'd been invited to. This was a chance for me to use my profile to have a lasting legacy.

I chose these girls in particular to be part of the programme simply because I believed they had what it took to go all the way. I had 20 years of training and competing as a female runner behind me and I wanted to share that with other people. After the first training camp in South Africa we replicated the same process in Australia, Spain and India – where a group attended the 2010 Commonwealth Games in Delhi and supported several athletes by taking them too. I had 65 athletes go through the programme over the next 10 years who went on to earn 22 medals at Commonwealth, European or global level. Two girls even competed in the 2012 Olympic Games. What an incredible achievement. I was so proud of every one.

The one thing I wanted was a sporting legacy and to inspire more girls to run the 800m and 1500m. It's another thing I feel extremely proud of now, watching athletics today with the current crop of world-class female middle distance runners. I still believe it takes one person to pave the way and make a difference and I hope I was the one that started that for others to follow.

Over the next decade I started a company called 'Kelly Holmes Education' which included On Camp With Kelly and a scheme called 'Future Stars With Kelly' which was for younger athletes and their coaches. I set up other mentoring and education programmes in the Isle of Man, Gateshead Academy and Jaguar Academy of Sport where numerous other athletes started, still competing to this day. To say I am proud of what I started way before I 'made it big' is an understatement, I just wish I could remind myself more often.

Sadly, however, running On Camp With Kelly for 10 years was yet another reason why I didn't come out during a time when my mental health was suffering again. I used to see so much homophobia in the media and crazy accusations of all sorts against members of the community who decided to work with young people of the same sex. It terrified me.

Acceptance of LGBT + people was still not great and I started to feel paranoia creeping in. I became convinced that if anyone found out I was gay they would think differently about me taking the girls away to training camps. I seriously thought that if anyone suggested something weird was happening or ever accused me of being untoward rather than just giving my hard work, commitment, time and energy, I would want to kill myself.

The sad thing is that people probably wouldn't have thought that at all, I was just so paranoid, I always expected the worst. That's how closeted and fearful the army and society had made me over the years.

Sexuality is such a big part of who you are. It shouldn't define you but if you hide the person you are, you're not fully living and it can have a detrimental effect on your personality and thought processes – it eventually invades your complete headspace. Living with a secret like that is like waiting for a ticking time-bomb to explode. I kept my secret so I could achieve the things I wanted to with those wonderful young athletes.

I've stayed in touch with some of them and I'm even planning a 20-year reunion of the first OCWK bunch next year. I know it will feel so good to finally feel free to be myself around them without fear or paranoia.

* * * * *

Ironically it wasn't On Camp With Kelly that started the rumour mill turning when I got back to South Africa after my golden summer, but another friendship. Amy was a member of the British Olympic Association support team who travelled with the athletes to training camps and stayed with us in the Olympic village while the Games were on. I got on well with all of them but Amy and I in particular became mates during the holding camp in Cyprus.

After the Games, I was writing one of my first books and she came over to South Africa to stay and do some work with me. It was good to have a friendly face around after all the chaos of the summer and she needed a break from it all too. We weren't in a romantic relationship, we were just mates, so I never thought twice about hanging out with her. I was probably busy worrying what people would think about On Camp With Kelly instead!

Then one day a message reached me from my agent in the UK that a newspaper back home had a photo of Amy and me together and they would be running it at the weekend. They said they understood we had "become very close" and asked whether I wanted to comment on the nature of the relationship. I was furious. They couldn't even spell out exactly what they were suggesting but they were going to put it out there for all to see. It was no one else's business.

For a start, there was nothing going on between me and Amy, and secondly, how could they possibly have a photograph of us? I felt totally violated. Had they been following me around even thousands of miles away in South Africa? We decided not to respond to the clear innuendo they were drawing because I didn't want to get into a war with a newspaper in case they went harder on me – so far, everyone had been nothing but kind and supportive since my Olympic success.

The press seemed to see me as a national treasure one day but wouldn't care about my feelings at all when they saw an opportunity for a good headline. It just goes to show how much the media has changed in the last 20 years. If you tried to out someone in a newspaper now you'd be in big trouble, but somehow back then it was fair game.

A story appeared alongside a pixelated picture of me and Amy sitting up on a rocky outcrop at the beach. The headline was 'Kelly: My Rock'. I was laughing as I read it:

'THIS is the 'rock' behind Olympic heroine Kelly Holmes,' it said. The article continued by insinuating we were together, claiming we were staying in a one-bedroom apartment, when in fact we were staying in my three-bedroom apartment. Then they dragged up the Maria Mutola rumours again.

It went on: 'Last night, a source said: "Kelly couldn't be happier. In the summer she pushed on to the next level in her career. Now Amy has helped her push on as a person". What a load of rubbish!

All the bad memories following the rumours about Maria and I came flooding back. This story was much more prominent than that one too, and it totally twisted everything.

The fact is, they should have never run that story, it was clearly a thinly-veiled attempt to out me, causing me anxiety and stress. What if my family hadn't already known about my sexuality? The other point is that when someone else is involved in any report, the papers are basically exposing them too, and I don't think that's right. As I have said before, for people who are not publicly 'out', it is no one else's right to try and make that huge step for them. The consequences could be completely damaging and, in some cases, people have taken their own lives under such enormous pressure.

* * * * *

Luckily, after that story, the rumours seemed to die down. I still had a season to do and was finding the motivation extremely hard. The papers soon went back to being nice to me when I announced my forthcoming official retirement from athletics in August 2005. The story became about my sporting achievements rather than my love life.

My last ever race was on British soil in Sheffield and it was such an emotional day. All my family came on a special bus for the event and there were flares, fireworks and five army helicopters flying in formation over the stadium as I finished my final straight in a black and gold outfit designed especially for me by Reebok.

It was the weirdest feeling knowing that it was all over and I no longer had that big goal to strive for, but I was also probably ready for a bit of a break from competing and some time out of the limelight.

Later on in 2004, I got an official letter from Downing Street telling me I'd been selected to appear in the Queen's New Year Honours List and I was going to be made a Dame Commander of the British Empire. I couldn't believe it, it was just so overwhelming to be honoured in that way, so much was happening to me it was incredible. I was the first woman to be given a damehood for sporting achievements and so again my family, Mum, Dad and my grandad all were so proud of me.

On March 9th, 2005, I was back off to Buckingham Palace to become 'Dame Kelly Holmes' and this time I made sure I wasn't hiding behind an awful hat. I had my hair done by Pat in a funky up-do and wore a slick, white tailored skirt suit by Jasper Conran.

There was one glitch though. When the organisers at the Palace were running through what I had to do when I went up to receive the honour, I expected them to tell me I would kneel before the Queen. A damehood is the female equivalent of a knighthood and the first thing you think of when you hear someone is knighted is kneeling before the monarch and being dubbed with a sword. I was gutted to hear that there was nothing quite so cool for the women who were awarded the same honour – we just had to go up there and curtsy!

I told the Lord Comptroller, who was explaining the protocol, that I wanted to kneel in front of my Queen to get the honour and he almost had a heart attack. It would have been the kind of break from protocol that probably would have caused total chaos, so when it was my turn I dutifully curtsied and accepted my medal with great pride.

I don't know if the Queen recognised me but, years later, I went to the racing at Royal Ascot and she addressed me as 'Dame Kelly'. We had a little chat about how we were both wearing the same colour blue that day and joked that it must be good luck for her horse that was racing so I think she knew who I was!

A bit later that year, I did something totally out of character and swapped my spikes for skates when I took on the challenge of appearing as a celebrity contestant on ITV's *Dancing On Ice*. I'm not sure what made me do it now because I've never really been a dancer but compared with some of the things I was asked to do, it felt like it would suit me because I could approach it like a sport. Unfortunately for my partner Todd Sand I didn't take to it quite as naturally as I did running!

My competitive spirit was in full force but I'd gone from being the gold medallist to struggling to keep up with the spins and heel-toes in the rink. It was hugely frustrating not being able to excel and be the best but I enjoyed the challenge and I ended up staying in for five weeks before I got booted off. The other issue is that I didn't understand the TV world and found it really hard to 'play the game' so I probably didn't show the best of myself at that time. I was also always so tense and on guard that I didn't allow myself to have fun. Looking back on my transition from sport, I found it extremely hard.

What I have learnt about myself is that, if I know how to do something then I am so confident, but when put outside my comfort zone I can get extremely anxious of showing myself up, feeling not good enough or embarrassed of what people might think.

I get asked all the time whether I would do *Strictly* or *I'm A Celebrity Get Me Out Of Here* or any of the other reality TV shows and, up until now, I've always said no but since coming out I do feel like I have a new lease of life, so never say never. If the time was right, you never know you might see me back on telly in a sequin outfit.

No title can make you better than anyone else but it can mean that you become established for more than just one thing. My damehood has opened doors, that I know for sure. But it has also given me a voice to speak up for the causes that are close to me.

Since 2005 I have been given even more honours and titles. Firstly, I have received around 12 honorary doctorates and fellowships and then I was made an Honorary Colonel in the British Army in 2018, so with my MBE for services to the British Army, my official title is now Colonel Dame Kelly Holmes MBE (mili)! Who would have thought that a mixed-raced girl with an afro from Kent would do so well?

After the Damehood I once again started getting more and more requests for interviews and TV appearances. I said no to a lot of them but when the call came from Piers Morgan's *Life Stories*, I knew I had to consider it. It was a bit like a modern-day rite of passage like *This Is Your Life* in the old days with the big red book.

Having opened up more about my past through my work with the DKH Trust and my mental health initiatives, I felt like now might be my time to tell my story. So long as I didn't have to talk about my personal relationships I could keep my sexuality out of it and hopefully just tell the inspiring story of how I got to where I am.

It was a huge milestone for me to feel confident enough to do it. I'd grown so much since that shy girl who appeared on Parky fresh back from Athens. Surely that was a good thing? Mum didn't agree.

"I don't think you should do it," she said, when I told her. "You're going to make me look like a terrible mother, why would you want to air your dirty laundry in public like that?"

She feared that when people heard about me being put in a children's home and then finding out about Lisa and Danny when I was a teenager, people would judge her and our family and people would gossip about us. But I didn't see it like that, and her reaction made me even more determined to do it because I had a right to tell my own story.

I accepted the offer and although I was nervous as hell, I got through it and did myself proud. I even appeared on the episode after Roger Moore, James Bond of all people. I was up there with 007! I had no regrets about doing it but it did cause a rift between me and Mum again and it took us months to get back on good terms.

It's easy to have regrets about arguments you have with loved ones after they have gone and to regret the time wasted by being in a rift with them but we are only human and I'm glad I stuck to my guns because, in hindsight, it was something I needed to do for myself. I hope deep down, in some way, Mum was proud I was strong enough to fight for it.

15

—

Champion in
My Corner

ONCE AN ATHLETE, ALWAYS AN ATHLETE, I SAY, AND sometimes there are no exceptions, even when you're competing with the Royal Family! At least that was the case when I played none other than the Princess of Wales at noughts and crosses, when she visited one of my charities young people programmes in Bristol with The Royal Foundation. It was a huge day and validation of the great work my charity the Dame Kelly Holmes Trust does to transform young people's lives and so exciting for my amazing Trust team, the schools, and the young people involved.

I've always wanted to inspire young athletes to achieve greatness but while that's a huge passion of mine, there are many kids out there who may not be cut out for a sporting career who also need help, guidance, and inspiration to succeed.

I think, because of my own background, I was always determined that if I ever got the right platform, I would also work hard to give those underprivileged kids opportunities outside of the sporting world.

I've done so much charity work over the years and I think it's really important for people in the public eye to do so. Not for money or gratitude but for love and compassion. I have also had numerous roles that I fought for myself. I was Ambassador for the Youth Sports Trust, National School Sports Champion under Gordon Brown's Government for three years, and I have supported cancer charities, military charities and mental health initiatives over the years. But I'm most proud of my own charity – the Dame Kelly Holmes Trust.

Sitting in a conference room at Bramall Lane football ground in Sheffield earlier this year, it hit me just what we have achieved and I felt an enormous sense of pride. My trust is now 15 years old and there in front of me in that room were all these young people and athletes that had been a part of it.

But how did it all start?

Well, if you look at the statistics on the life chances for children who have been in care and grown up in areas of deprivation or from underprivileged backgrounds, they are far more likely to end up struggling in adulthood with unemployment, addiction problems, mental health issues and even crime.

I was no genius at school and struggled to find my place in the world. It was only really because I happened to have people who believed in me like Miss Page and the inspiring careers officers from the recruitment office in Tunbridge Wells that I managed to get myself on track and have a successful career. When I look back at my life, it could have turned out so differently and, in a way, I am just so lucky my talent for running was identified.

I founded the Dame Kelly Holmes Trust in 2008, with the target of giving young people with challenging backgrounds a chance to believe they had a brighter future. The idea was to assign each of them a mentor who would believe in them, no matter where they came from and no matter what their dream.

After I retired from athletics, I knew of other sports people who reached the end of their careers and also were searching for a purpose in life. Retiring from any kind of intense career is tough because you get a sense of lost identity that can make you question your worth or positioning in society. My idea was to put these people together with the children who needed that support and to let them work together. It was a huge success.

At first, setting up a charity seemed like a mountain to climb but I knew it could work, so I started contacting former athletes I knew from my competing days and I was amazed at how many were keen to come on board. I registered the Trust as a charity and employed a tiny team of admin and organisational staff to begin with, funding it out of my own pocket. The Trust was born.

We targeted schools in deprived areas, young offender institutions, social services, Jobcentre Plus, youth clubs – anywhere we thought could give us access to vulnerable young people who needed our help. Kids from across the country who had been in care, or suffered difficult family situations, grown up in areas of deprivation or been young carers themselves all started to join our programmes.

Some of them had been in trouble with the police or started to go off the rails and others were just completely lacking in confidence from trauma they'd experienced as children. Some amazing organisations like football clubs lent their spaces for free so we could arrange days for groups of kids to meet up for workshops and training sessions and just to meet other people like themselves so they felt less alone.

It was amazing to watch them gradually come out of their shells and tell us about what had brought them to us. I remember one young boy whose mum had been in and out of prison for most of his life so he'd been from home to home, never able to settle properly or focus on his studies or what he wanted from his own life. It turned out he actually had loads of ideas for businesses and was a budding young entrepreneur but he just had no capital and no direction so the trust helped him to build a business plan, apply for grants and set himself up in a way he never could have done by himself. He managed to get a home of his own and the kind of stability he'd craved all his life. There were hundreds of stories like his and every one I heard was different.

As I heard their stories, I was taken right back to my feelings of fear, abandonment and displacement all those years ago and probably for the first time in my adult life I spoke openly about what happened to me too. They were always astonished to hear my background and how I started out in life and I think hearing how I managed to make such a success of my life from such humble beginnings gave them the inspiration to want to do it for themselves too.

I'm extremely proud of my trust and everyone who has ever worked with us throughout the years, the teachers, carers, social workers, sponsors, businesses and of course the young people and so grateful to every athlete who has become a mentor, working on our programmes or running the sessions. I'm the person who started the Trust but they are the people that now continue my legacy and they make my heart feel so warm.

Over the last 15 years, we have helped thousands of young people through various programmes helping many on their road to success and self-confidence. After my gold medals, along with On Camp With Kelly, it's probably one of my proudest achievements.

* * * * *

While I was building the charity those first few years it was a really inspirational time because I'd also worked on the London 2012 Olympic bid and now that was coming to fruition, so I was involved in the preparations for that. I had mentored young athletes who would later go through the selection process for Team GB.

Finally I was going to an Olympic Games with no worries about bringing my own medals home – my only responsibility was giving our brilliant athletes support and belief and to create a wonderful sporting legacy for the nation.

The two weeks in August 2012 certainly didn't disappoint. The opening ceremony directed by Danny Boyle was incredible and made me so proud to watch. It was a celebration not only of sport but of our nation, its people, the military, the NHS, Shakespeare, Elgar, the Beatles and all that makes us who we are. The fact 27 million people watched it on telly shows what an enormous moment it was for us as a nation and I will never forget it.

I was selected as an ambassador of the Games along with six other sporting legends. Our biggest role was to be inspirational figures to the younger generation but we also had the honour of handing the torches to seven young athletes who would go on to light the Olympic cauldron at the opening ceremony to start London 2012 – another 'pinch-me' moment.

That same year, I received another sign from the universe that I had to follow. Back in Hildenborough, I'd always had this dream of buying the little sweet shop where I'd worked as a teenager before I joined the army. I always remembered the local people coming in to chat and they were some of my happiest memories, being a part of that community. I'd tried to buy it before but the timing and the price had never been right. But in 2012, after the Olympics, I got a call from the estate agents telling me it was up for sale again.

I'd always told myself that if it ever became available when I was older and I had the money, I would buy it. So that's what I did! Most people impulse-buy expensive shoes or a car but I got myself a building in the heart of a sunny Kent village without much of a plan of what I was going to do with it. I quickly decided I wanted to turn it into a little café, a meeting place for the community where they could come together and socialise.

What I didn't realise when I bought it, was that it was going to take a lot of work, time, energy and money. But I do like a project, and a challenge, so I wasn't deterred. I got in contractors and builders, structural engineers and set about knocking down the walls of the building on Florence Place. I started to create a massive 100-seater coffee house, more fitting for a trendy London street than a blink-and-you-miss-it rural village. It was a labour of love – and stress – but after a year of being project manager, hod carrier, foreman and tea-maker on the site of the old sweet shop, in 2014, finally it was ready to open its doors to the public.

I christened it Café 1809 after my bib number in Athens. I also had tattooed *Run 1809* on my foot so I could never forget those four special digits. I was so proud of everything. The decor, which I designed with a local guy, featured cool industrial furniture, steel beams and lighting. In the apex roof were huge photos of me crossing the finishing line in Athens. I held interviews and employed some young people from the local community as waiting staff and picked out trendy uniforms. I was still such a stickler for ironing from my army days. I would do a joke inspection when they came in and even taught some of them to iron – yes, really! I remember one girl was once running late and came in looking like she'd just picked the shirt up off the floor and slung it on. I didn't shout, I just gave her 'the look' and sent her home to change it. She came back with it all ironed, fit for an army inspection.

The café was my pride and joy and it felt like home. There was something so special about transforming that building where I'd grafted as a kid to save the money to buy my parents our first tumble dryer then, when I was 16, a scooter and finally my first car. It felt like I'd properly come home to my community and given them something back.

Everyone in Hildenborough knew me. They would come into the café sometimes for a cup of tea or lunch, but more importantly just for a chat to see how things were going. I would get to know the old dears who popped in after getting a perm; the kids who visited on their way home from school or the mums with pushchairs trying to get their babies to sleep as they drank endless coffee. Kerrie had her own little company making amazing cakes and bakes by that point, so I sold them from the counter to make her a bit of extra cash too.

I could get from home to work in less than five minutes and I had a manager who would look after 1809 when I needed to be off travelling for OCWK or the Trust. It felt like the perfect balance between my own little project and giving something back in a wider sense.

The only problem with being back in the heart of the village, in a place where people go to gossip was that everyone knew everyone else's business! At that time I was fully convinced I was the Only Gay In The Village like Dafydd in the sketch show *Little Britain* by Matt Lucas and David Walliams. I would joke about it with my friends. Looking back I'm sure some people knew I was gay and others probably either had no clue or didn't care either way but nonetheless I kept my personal life very private.

The most important relationships to me at that time, though, were my friends and family. Kev, Stuart, Lisa, Danny and Penny all still live in Kent so being able to see my siblings and my nieces and nephews as much as I wanted was a huge bonus. Plus Mum and Dad were around the corner so I had all my loved ones in one place – what more could I want?

16

Broken Hearted

EVER SINCE I WAS SMALL, I'VE BEEN TERRIFIED OF death. I hate ageing, the thought of being old and I can't stand hospitals or being ill. I used to lie awake at night worrying about something happening to one of my parents and my worst nightmare has always been contemplating when one of them might get ill or worse, die. I think it goes back to being a child and being scared of losing Mum again after she left me in the children's home or when I was growing up feeling that she was my one constant. My ultimate fear was that one day I would have to live without her.

One bonus of having a young mum was that I always assumed we would have years and years together. Now I was back in Kent and we could see one another as often as we wanted, it felt like we would have plenty of time to make up for those lost years. After all, her mum, my nan Elsie lived until she was 98!

Towards the end of 2014, I had gone around to her bungalow after her shift at the hospital and she was complaining of a back ache, which she'd never mentioned before. She was an active woman who'd had jobs requiring her to be on her feet all day for years and never complained before. She seemed to be run down and exhausted, which wasn't like her.

Me being me, I thought she must have just pulled a muscle so I started massaging her over the course of a couple of weeks. But the pain wasn't relenting and as she was working at a hospital anyway, I persuaded her to go to the doctor.

For months she said she was fine and it was just old age catching up with her but she was only 61, so I kept nagging her. I knew from my own experience with my many sporting injuries that the longer you leave a niggle without getting it checked out, the worse it will get. Mum was adamant, though, and carried on as normal. When she did go to the GP, they didn't think it was anything serious so we all agreed to just keep an eye on her.

As she seemed to be struggling a bit, I tried to see Mum as much as I could and I would often go over to the bungalow where she was living with Penny and order a Chinese while we watched telly. She loved sweet and sour chicken balls and egg fried rice with chips. I always tried to get her to change her order to something more adventurous but she would say: "I know what I like," and I would laugh.

We would watch crap TV for hours and sometimes, if I wanted company, I would sleep on her sofa even though I had a five-bedroom house up the road. By now, we had got past our row about Piers Morgan and things were back to normal. We were soon seeing each other almost every day when I was in Kent. There was something special about time spent with her on my own.

Then one day, when Mum came over, she said that she'd spoken to one of the consultants at work who suggested that she have a scan to see what was causing her back pain. Immediately I went into panic mode. A scan didn't sound like good news. I'd had enough of them myself to know they usually pick up a problem and as Mum was a 61-year-old woman and not an elite athlete, I guessed it would pick up something more serious than a muscle injury.

As it turned out, the scan was inconclusive so the doctor insisted on some specialist blood tests and the following week asked Mum back in for the results, and to take someone with her. Kevin, Stuart, Penny and I all went. We knew they wouldn't have called her in if there was nothing to worry about. I remember sitting in the cramped little doctor's office as he told us Mum had a rare form of cancer called myeloma, a sort of lymphoma that attacks the blood cells and bone marrow. We all listened in stunned silence as he said those words you dread hearing: "It's incurable."

I felt my heart start to race. I felt sick rising in my stomach but I knew I had to keep a cool head. I was already thinking about how we could get her to see the best doctors and what I could do to help – to keep her alive. I just couldn't even bear to think about life without her – I couldn't let it happen. But before I could speak, the doctor said that while there was no cure, there was treatment Mum could have and that she could have it there at Pembury and at Maidstone Hospital down the road. So we all agreed she would start the treatment as soon as possible to give herself the best chance of extending her life for as long as possible.

Back home, Mum tried to put on a brave face and we talked about dividing up the hospital appointments and trips to the pharmacy to collect the tons of different pills she'd been prescribed.

Penny would look after her at home while she was off work and we would take it in turns to take her for her chemotherapy which she was due to start straight away. She had a blood transfusion too, to try and kickstart the production of new healthy blood cells and regenerate her bone marrow. It was a huge shock to get the diagnosis but I think we were all just so focused on making sure the treatments available worked, we pulled together as a family and hoped for the best.

Even though Mum worked in a hospital, she hated being a patient. After years of being a nursing assistant, it felt unnatural for her to be on the receiving end of the poking and prodding, plus it was hard for her to be seen in a weak and vulnerable state by her colleagues. I was amazed at how brave she was. As she sat shivering with the chemo coursing through her veins, she never complained. (I also couldn't believe the amount of drugs cancer patients have to take, I can't even take a Benadryl without suffering from the side effects!).

Remarkably after that first round of chemo, further blood tests showed it had worked and she was significantly stronger than she'd been before. Her blood was regenerating and the cancer seemed to be losing its battle with the drugs. "I told you I'd be okay," she told me, as though I'd been fussing over nothing. Within a couple of months, she was back working on the X-ray ward. We couldn't believe it.

For a while she seemed much stronger and life went back to normal but the following year, she began to complain of exhaustion, pain and tiredness again.

More tests showed the cancer was back with a vengeance. I remember standing by the bed squeezing her hand as she had a painful marrow extraction from her pelvis – that was brutal! I knew from the look on her face and the pain she was in that day that she knew it was serious. Months passed and she underwent more chemo and her prescriptions from the pharmacy seemed to come in bigger bags every week. She had to give up work permanently and gradually found it harder to move around.

One morning, two years after the diagnosis, I arrived at the bungalow early in the morning and Mum didn't even have the strength to get out of bed and use the bathroom. Her complexion was grey and she looked really unwell. I got her to the toilet and she collapsed. I panicked and called an ambulance to take her into hospital.

It was the first of two long stints on a ward. She was suffering from pneumonia which had hit her hard because her immune system was so low. Seeing Mum like that was awful. The next few months she was in and out and eventually Dr Wyke, her consultant, suggested she go to a hospital in Maidstone for some tests and to see if they could do anything.

"What's the point of me being here if I'm just in and out of hospitals," Mum cried. "I just want to be at home and to see my chickens."

On the June 14th, 2017, the doctor gave us the result of her latest tests and confirmed that she only had months to live. Once again we were all there when she got the news and we were in total shock. I could see the boys trying to be brave. I felt somehow as the eldest that I should be the strong one. In a situation like that it's hard not to let the emotions get the better of you though. I can't remember if I cried there and then, but I know when I got back home that night I was a wreck. The thought of being without Mum was just unbearable. I wasn't ready to lose her.

* * * * *

After weeks of sitting at Mum's side in the hospital, she'd finally turned a corner and the doctors had even allowed her to go home to the bungalow I'd bought for her a few years earlier. She'd been begging to get off the ward since the moment she was admitted because she hated being the one that needed looking after – that was *her* job.

Mum and I got closer than ever during that time she was on the ward. I would get up early and cycle from my place in Hildenborough across to the hospital in time to spend the day sitting at her side.

We would laugh and joke about her times working in the hospital. She would tell funny stories about giving elderly patients enemas and then them farting and giving her a shower! It was also the same hospital where she'd had me years earlier and we would talk about my younger days too, though she always found it hard to speak about the time we were on our own, before Mick and the rest of the family came along.

Most of all, she just wanted to get back to her own home. So when there was a break in her chemotherapy and the doctors deemed she was well enough to leave, we were over the moon. Penny was living in the bungalow and could look after her while she was there and the rest of us would take turns to visit. Even Dad was on hand to help out when we needed him. After all those years and so much water under the bridge he still cared so much for Mum, you could see it.

I'd been umming and ahhing over whether to go away on a short break to Greece with a girl I'd been seeing to get some sunshine and a bit of a break from all the hospital visits. When she was given the green light to go home, Mum was adamant that I should go. "Just go and enjoy yourself," she said. "I'll be fine."

Running through the airport in a blind panic, I could feel my heart racing. I just needed to get on a plane and get home as soon as I could. I'd been in Greece for less than 48 hours when Kevin had called. "Something's happened, Mum's back in hospital," he said. "You need to come back."

It wasn't clear on that phone call exactly what he meant but I knew straight away that I needed to get on a flight home. The problem was that the villa I was in was on a little island; a boat ride away from the mainland and where the airport was – and the crossings were few and far between. I felt totally helpless as I desperately tried to think of how I could get back. I actually spoke to my mum, telling her to hang on as I was on my way back. But there was nothing I could do. It was nine hours before I could get to the airport and hopefully get onto a plane.

In a total panic, I ran to the bathroom and locked myself in, I picked up some nails scissors as I had 11 years ago and cut myself on the leg. What the hell was I doing? I was going back years in my recovery from self-harm. I wanted to take away the pain I thought my mum was in, but I had a sudden revelation that no matter how deep the cut, Mum would still be lying in a hospital bed potentially dying and I would still be here. The phone rang again and I rushed out in hope of some better news, but my greatest fear became true. Stuart told me Mother Dear had died.

My world suddenly went into slow motion and I felt a physical pain tear through my body as though someone was actually reaching into my chest and ripping my heart in two. All I could think was 'no, don't let it be true'. But it was.

By the time I got to the hospital, Mum was in the chapel of rest. It turned out that the morning I'd left, she hadn't got out of bed as usual, and Penny had struggled to wake her. She had called Kev and Stu, and they tried to take her to the bathroom but Mum didn't even have the strength to stand and had to use the commode left there since the last bad turn she'd had. Mum lost consciousness in the ambulance and passed away soon after she got to hospital.

As I went into the room where she was peacefully laid out, I couldn't believe she'd actually gone as I held her hand and kissed her on the head, speaking to her for the last time, telling her I loved her, telling her I was sorry I hadn't been there.

She was only 65, it was so unfair. Our relationship in those last few years had become closer and better than ever. That's the thing about losing people you love, it's so finite you don't just lose a person, you lose a part of yourself.

Mum was the most important person in my life since I was a baby and, despite all of our ups and downs, I felt like our souls were bonded together. It wasn't just that she was my only full blood relative, but it was that it was just us in the beginning, the only person who had been there through my entire life. I genuinely feel like the part of me that died that day will never come back.

After Mum died I barely functioned. For three weeks I could only sort funeral arrangements. I stopped work as I was so consumed with grief. I missed Mum so much that I found it hard to do anything. I know some people need to throw themselves back into routine but I couldn't. It was one of those critical moments in my life when I truly needed my friends and family the most.

17

—

Letting Her Go

IN THE DARKEST OF TIMES YOU HAVE TO FOCUS ON
the things you have control over and one of those, for me, was
the way we would say goodbye to Mum. It was three years from
diagnosis to her passing away and one thing I am grateful for is
that we did have plenty of time to talk about exactly what she
wanted for her funeral.

Having grown up in Hildenborough village you seemed to
know everyone and sadly, one of the ladies I had known for
years died. Earlier in 2017 we attended her funeral and getting
there late, we sat at the back of the crematorium.

When Mother Dear saw the coffin, a big wooden box, she
said: "I don't want one like that." I didn't know what other kinds
of coffins there were, but she whispered, "put me in a wicker
casket, otherwise I am coming back to haunt you!"

We were both laughing as I told her to stop being stupid and
to 'ssshhh!'

I had previously had a really hard conversation with her

about wanting to be cremated, not buried. If I have any advice to anyone going through a similar traumatic experience, please have the hardest conversations you will ever have with a loved one about what their wishes are. To be honest, out of all the heartache, this is one thing I am so happy I did; knowing what she wanted.

On the morning of my mum's funeral, I went to my hairdresser Luci, who had been doing my hair for years. As I sat in the chair I asked her to shave my head on one side just leaving a bit more length on the top. It was the look I'd always wanted but avoided in favour of braids or a straightened bob through the years. It sounds like a stereotype but I was convinced if someone saw me with an undercut they would take that as a sign I was gay. But now Mum was gone, I didn't care what anyone thought.

In the years before she left us, Mum would often say how much she wished I could just be open about who I was and live my life without caring so much about what other people thought. She was desperate for me to be happy and to be myself.

Now, in a little act of defiance, and in tribute to her, that was what I decided to do. There was a bloody long way to go, but looking back, that was the first step on my five-year journey to being me.

You hear about people from the LGBTQIA+ community who wait until their parents pass away to come out because they feel like they would be hurt or ashamed of them but, for me, it was the other way around. Mum wanted that freedom for me and now I felt like I owed it to us both to try to free myself from the shackles that had held me for so long.

For the funeral arrangements, I made sure Mum's wishes were adhered to and that each of us chose a song that was special to us. Mine was *This Woman's Work* by Kate Bush. The lyrics are so

Honoured
Wearing black – my comfort colour – as I meet the Queen at Buckingham Palace in 2004 and (below) receiving my DBE with Grandad Geoff and my dad Mick

We've done it!
(Above) celebrating in 2005 as London wins the right to host the Olympic Games in 2012

Giving back
On Camp With Kelly, 2004 to 2014. Mentoring before it was trendy

Always with us (Left) at Mother Dear's bench with Kev, Penny and Stu and (above) Kev, Danny and Stu – all grown up now

Special bond With my sister Lisa

I love you Dad At his beloved Tonbridge FC

We are family My wonderful nieces and nephews who I hope will always understand acceptance. Numbered in birth order so I don't lose track! (Above) nieces 5,6,4, 7 and nephews 2 and 1 and (right) nieces 2,1,8,3

Forever friends Enjoying the company of Debs, Kerrie, Lara and Kim – 42 years together

Four-legged family
(Above, left) 'The Boys' (without Fudge) had their own reality show during lockdown. (Right) Mum came back... as a donkey?!

Simply the best
My lockdown antics as Tina Turner

Freedom is my voice On stage in Trafalgar Square for Pride 2023 – finally free to be me

You can do it Gok Wan gave me confidence and (right) Alan Carr calmed my nerves

Finding the real me With Kelly Hoppen and (right) Dr Tania Pilley, who helped me so much

Telling the world my story Filming the *Kelly Holmes: Being Me* documentary

On parade Enjoying the Trooping of the Colour as an Honorary Colonel

Palace party At the Platinum Jubilee celebrations with Sally Gunnell and co

Read all about it With Emeli Sandé (above) and (right) with Dawn Butler and Linda Riley

Troopers With some of my Military in Motion gang. They gave me a lifeline during lockdown

Support With Kerrie in 2021 during my burnout (left) and (right) the Princess of Wales visiting a Dame Kelly Holmes Trust project in Bristol, with The Royal Foundation

The inner circle clan If you know, you know

New experiences
Learning to be
Loose with these
wonderful women

Righting the wrongs With veterans in the
House of Commons, after the Prime Minister's
apology for the mistreatment and unethical,
historical ban on LGBT serving personnel

Queuing for the Queen...
And meeting a man named
John (right). Embracing the
colours at The Castro (above)

With Lou When you can finally feel free, you can be yourself and happy!

Athena Effect (Bottom left) On a mission to make a difference

Panto Oh, yes I did! Here I am as Ringmistress Olympia in the panto production *Goldilocks and the Three Bears*

full of emotion and the words describe exactly how I felt during the time she was ill.

I know you've got a little life in you left,
I know you've got a lotta strength left,
I should be cryin' but I just can't let it show,
I should be hopin' but I can't stop thinkin',
All the things we should've said that are never said,
All the things we should've done that we never did,
All the things we should've given, but I didn't.
Oh darlin', make it go,
Make it go away,
Give me these moments,
Give them back to me.

I knew that as soon as I heard the first bars of it I would be a complete wreck and I was. I'd also agreed, as the oldest, to do a reading on behalf of the four of us kids. I regularly spoke to huge rooms full of people for my work because I was a motivational speaker, but now, the thought of standing in front of a room of people while I was so emotional, filled me with dread.

On the morning of the funeral, dressed in black, along with Kev, Stu and Penny, six of us carried the wicker casket on our shoulders into the crematorium, to say our final goodbyes. After the humanist did her address, I read – or tried to read – a poem I'd written for Mum, mentioning all the happy things I remembered about her.

I wanted to include her love of nature, birds and horses and how special she was to me. Standing in front of the congregation, the tears came and I swallowed hard, choking them back as I was determined to read the poem for her.

My heart gallops like a racehorse charging down the furlong,
My head pounds like the beat of a drum,
My body falters with every walking step as my eyes fill and blur,
My heart skips a beat each time I breathe,
The growl in my voice has lost its bark,
but I lie with the sound of your voice around me
like the morning lark,
I think I can see you but then you disappear,
like a piece of my heart that went when yours stopped.
I can't believe you are gone but the biggest gift you gave me
was the strength of your mind to carry on.

One of the things that really hits my core, the same as when my grandparents all passed, is that when the curtain slowly surrounds the coffin or it's taken away, that's it. But one thing that gives me peace with my Mother Dear passing is that I know she would have at least been happy with her send-off.

When I look back at that day, I think we made Mum proud. But as time went on, in moments of crises, grief can drive us to act out of character. I believe massive change in our lives can also help us to connect with our inner spirit; one we may not even know is there.

Soon after the funeral I got a tattoo of a jigsaw puzzle piece over my chest to symbolise what I feel is a missing piece of my heart alongside a clock face to show that there's no time for healing and an eye to show I will always be searching for her.

People have asked me in recent times why I started getting tattoos. They were around for me long before my mum passed away. Mine actually started when I was a young recruit in the army. One of my first rebellions was going with some of the other girls to this house of a guy who did tattoos. We ended up getting a tiny tattoo on our hips of different fruits! I got a bloody strawberry – why?! I didn't realise how tattoos would have a deeper meaning as I got older. For me they are an expression of my thoughts, a show of identity and purpose, to signify a moment in time, a memory or a belief.

After the strawberry, they became more prominent for me when I was an athlete; I loved the thought of having powerful words on my body permanently. Before my Olympic wins I had already experienced success in my army career which was a fight for identity, purpose and respect. I also had success as an athlete, both in the military and in world athletics, so I found a Chinese symbol – that used to be the in-thing in the '90s – the meaning was 'Strength and Power'. It was just a small insignia on my right shoulder. Of course, I thought I was invincible back then!

As time went on, I left the army and had my battles with injuries on the track as well as health issues and gynaecological problems (bloody periods and women's issues drove me crazy – just another setback I didn't need). So I added another Chinese symbol underneath that translated to 'Will to Win'. Little did I know it would later become my mantra!

In a strange twist of fate a year after my Olympic double, I was visiting China for an awards ceremony. After finishing a run, a local man stopped me in the street and pointed at the tattoo. There was no way on this earth he knew who I was as he swept up the pathway outside his humble little shack.

I thought it was a bizarre moment because when I asked him what it meant (hoping he wouldn't say something completely unrelated) he spoke in very broken English 'extraordinary victory'. I was stunned! Still processing what I had achieved the year before, it felt like another sign to me and always makes me believe that my gold medals were meant to be.

I believe Mother Dear comes to me in certain ways when I need her and to give me strength.

After she passed away, I began seeing butterflies at the most unusual times; one even landed on my shorts when I was on a charity trip to Malawi. We had just pulled into the shore after kayaking on Lake Malawi. I was lying in the sun, wishing I could have called Mum and showed her where I was, like I used to every time I was away, when a butterfly came towards me. A single butterfly. It hovered above me before landing on my shorts. I thought it was going to just fly off but it didn't, I swear it stayed there for 10 minutes and I even had time to take a photo of it. That's why my next tattoo was a butterfly above the puzzle piece, another reminder she is always here.

Tattoos for me have become more than just art or an act of rebellion to conforming, they have become symbolic of my life journey. Each time I have got a tattoo (apart from the bloody strawberry I got on my hip in the army!) it has been about a reflection of my state of mind or a stage in my life that has had some life changing impact.

Thinking back on my horrific night without sleep, pinning my body in my bed whilst my spirit was wandering down to the kitchen to reach for the knife drawer, I realised that I had a moment of power; a resistance to go downstairs in the midst of my deep despair.

I felt so emotional about that period of my journey I was compelled to get the word L;fe on the inside of my left wrist. I had the 'i' down as a semicolon, because it represents a personal strength to overcome internal struggles.

It's a reminder on my dark days that "I chose Life "

In the past five years I have added numerous tattoos that have been part of my own spiritual and mental health journey. They

symbolise many aspects and different stages of my life, like;
growth, healing, positivity, hope and life. I have a quote on my
arm which says:

> 'Strong enough to stand alone,
> Smart enough to know when I need help and
> Brave enough to ask for it'

I'd written it to remind me that even in the darkest of times,
through grief, there is always help out there. Maybe it can help
you too.

Three years after Mum died, I wrote:

*'Three years ago today, my mum 'Mother Dear' passed away.
That day was the worst time of my life. My heart broke in pieces.
That day was also the last time I self-harmed. I knew it would not
bring her back and it definitely would destroy me. Loss is horrendous! But we never talk about it – why? Everyone deals with
it in different ways, I cried for three weeks solid leading up to her
funeral, I became a bit of a recluse. My friends and family were
my lifeline.*

*The pain and loss is still there and I miss her so much but you
learn to deal with it as life carries on. I changed the day of Mother
Dear's funeral – I know I did. For me, probably for the better. I am
a private person to some degree. I know people probably wonder
exactly 'who I am' but I don't care anymore because I am who I
am! I am waiting for a butterfly to come down – maybe she is
sleeping. I want to be free like a beautiful butterfly but so far my
life, whilst glorious and special, has sometimes felt like being a
moth in a cocoon. I want to one day be free from this anguish but
I don't know how…*

'One of the hardest things about losing Mother Dear is that she is not around to see how I have changed my life, but what is important now is whilst I am walking on this earth, I must actually live my life. REST IN PEACE, MUM'

* * * * *

It wasn't just the type of coffin she wanted that Mum had told us about. Firstly, no way on earth did she want to be buried. "I'm claustrophobic," she said. "You won't know, you'll be dead!" I would joke. She was cremated. I wasn't taking the risk of her threats to come back and haunt me – no way!

In the later stages of her illness, she told me she dreamt of buying a camper van with her pension money and travelling around the country to visit some special places.

Unfortunately, by the time she had a chance to buy one, it was too late and she was far too poorly. So in the year after she died, Kevin, Stuart, Penny and I decided to make our own pilgrimages to each of the places and to scatter her ashes where she could rest in peace forever.

We started closer to home at the lake in Haysden Country Park. Mum used to go to walk her dogs over the years and one of her wishes that I had spoken to her about was to have a bench placed there in her memory. It had always been a place to enjoy the countryside, so we decided to take her back there too.

I called the local council and told them I wanted a bench dedicated to her, overlooking the lake where she felt so peaceful and they said we could. Mum also said she wanted, 'Take a pew and enjoy the view' as the inscription, so that's what we had engraved on a silver plaque. Now there are some little holders either side of the armrests where we can leave flowers when we visit.

Stuart, Clare, Kevin, Emma and Penny went down to the lake with the kids, but we had no idea what the protocol was for scattering ashes in a public place. What if there were some health and safety rules or we got caught? It sounds ridiculous now, but we were all giggling as I took the cardboard container with the ashes from the crematorium in, hiding it under my nephew Finlay's coat, and we scattered them like you would a Shake n' Vac!

We each took a handful and walked around the whole lake. What I couldn't believe was how much was left when we got back. I'd never had any idea the amount of ashes there would be.

The first road trip to scatter more of the ashes was to the New Forest, the place Mum wanted to go to most of all. She was a huge lover of horses and loved seeing the white horses in the forest roaming free on the open heathland. For this trip we all took our bikes which was a task in itself given we had all the kids, but it was a laugh as we went searching specifically for the white horses, not brown, black or grey, it had to be white! Sounds easy, but it was only after an hour of searching, and going round in circles we finally came across some.

We stood in a row and each took a handful to scatter. Just at that solemn moment, the wind whipped up. We all fell about laughing, wiping the ashes from our jackets and faces. It wasn't the perfect peaceful send-off I'd imagined but it was very much about doing it as a family and we were all there together, that was what mattered. That spot became a really special place for our family after that, and we still go back to visit. Three years later I wrote on my Instagram:

'Had an amazing day with my family down at the New Forest. My Mum 'Mother Dear' wanted to go there and I had told her I

would take her a couple of weeks after she came out of hospital for a break. But sadly she died before that. My family and I had gone down a couple of months after for her and found this wonderful place – Hatchet Pond.

'Three years since Mother Dear left us, we went again. Now there are wild horses, donkies, cows everywhere... this donkey befriended me, it stayed staring me out for ages and just didn't move! It even sneezed over me, it felt that comfortable. I had a good chat with it as I stared into its eyes. I know my Mother Dear is around in spirit, but as a bloody donkey??!'

Next stop on the ashes tour was the Isle Of Wight. We never went on holiday much as kids but I do remember one year Mum and Dad took us to the Isle of Wight for a proper seaside holiday. We stayed in a caravan park, went to Blackgang Chine or to Alum Bay to collect the multi-coloured sands, just like I'd imagined other families did or school kids had on end-of-year trips.

It was obviously a happy memory for Mum too because it was one of the places she wanted to go back to. Sadly she never got the chance but instead, the whole family and I piled into our cars and drove down to the ferry and booked caravans on a campsite for the weekend.

One night we decided to get a Chinese takeaway (Mum's favourite) in her honour, but first it was bingo! Penny always moaned that she never won anything but we all told her that we just had a feeling she was going to win and that Mum would help her. By some bizarre turn of events we were right – she hit the jackpot! With her winnings she treated us all to Mum's favourite: egg fried rice, sweet and sour chicken balls and chips.

The next day, the craziness continued. We went to the end of the pier to scatter her ashes. It was set to be another comedy scattering as we threw handfuls into the sea and, just like the New Forest, a gust of wind came from nowhere and the ashes ended up in our faces. We didn't mind though. We agreed Mum was probably having a laugh with us as she watched us spitting her out of our mouths.

I definitely knew she was around when, after having walked through the arcade back to the cars, I realised I had lost my glasses – yet again. I ran back to find them but couldn't. Thinking they were lost, I walked to the entrance just as Penny came in to find me. Out of the blue some young lad, who was playing on a slot machine, turned around and just handed me them. Penny and I stared at each other in disbelief; instantly we both knew it was Mum!

Almost a year after Mum died, with the last of her ashes still in the box, it was time to let her go. The final resting place we'd chosen was a place called Cleeve Hill in Gloucestershire. Mum had always wanted to go to the Cotswolds and Cleeve seemed perfect as it overlooked the famous Cheltenham racecourse.

Mum loved the races, hence the reference in my poem, and we knew she would be happy there, looking down on the gee-gees. After a three-hour journey, the weather was awful and, to cut a long story short, we had to head back home. It wasn't for another six months that just four of us returned and finally laid her to rest.

While we were travelling around, scattering Mum's ashes, it felt like the final chapter of her life was still ongoing. Once we had finished, I expected the heartache would all be over, but it wasn't. Having suffered from mental health problems in the past, I knew only too well what depression felt like, but this time it was different. While before my depression and anxiety and self-harm had seemed irrational in hindsight, this time it made perfect sense to me; I felt like the world was ending. I'd lost my mum, the person I loved most in the entire world, my one constant throughout life.

I went through the motions and focused on working, paying the bills and just praying that one day soon, things would feel better. Over the following 18 months, I still felt utterly consumed with grief; I missed Mum so much that I found it nearly impossible to go out with my friends and have fun or find joy in anything, really. Just when you think you've found ways to manage and move forward, things can take an unexpected turn and the world, and my life, was just about to go bonkers!

18

When the World
Stopped

"THEY'RE SAYING IT'S GETTING WORSE IN ENGLAND too, you know," said Kate as we chatted over dinner in a Manhattan restaurant in New York. "I read that hundreds of people are being taken to hospitals now."

I looked around us, and it was definitely quiet for a spot in the middle of the city that supposedly never sleeps. It was March 2020 and I'd taken a much-needed break from work for a few days to visit the Big Apple. Kate and I had dated for about six months the previous year, we'd split, but stayed good mates so she came along with me. We'd been planning the trip for ages. Now it didn't seem like quite such a good idea.

Around Christmas time we'd started hearing about some weird deadly virus in China that was killing people and there was no cure. They called it Coronavirus to begin with, then Covid-19 and it sounded like some crazy conspiracy theory from a disaster movie. I hadn't taken much notice of it to begin with but then I heard Brits from Wuhan, the town where people started falling sick, had been evacuated back to RAF Brize Norton and it seemed pretty serious.

Anyone coming back from China had to be quarantined, so we did check about flights and they were still going from London to New York and most places around the world. How bad could it be? Very bad, it turned out!

The first night we arrived in New York, we were looking around a packed Times Square. Then these messages started to appear on the huge billboards saying that Broadway was shutting. You could hear all the murmurs and saw the disbelief because people were actually queueing for the shows.

Over the next two days, our hotel restaurant announced it was closing; restaurants were boarded up and the streets were emptying. I'd taken a picture on the Manhattan Bridge with no one in sight and later, when I was sitting on the subway, it was completely empty. It was like a scene from a movie where suddenly they heard something awful was going to happen and everyone locked themselves indoors. What was so strange is that it all happened so damned quickly, it was eerie.

Back at the hotel I had a very uneasy feeling and started checking the news on my phone. That's when I saw there had been an announcement in the UK that they were planning to close the borders and stop people from outside Europe coming back – TOMORROW!

"We have to get to the airport and get on a flight," I panicked, already throwing my things into a bag. "No way I am getting stranded over here. I have work, the house and The Boys to get back to. Come on, let's go!"

We jumped in a yellow cab and dashed to JFK, desperately

trying to change our flights on the way. When we got there, it was chaos with people from all over the world panicking as they tried to get back home to their families. Thankfully we managed to get on an early flight. I called Dad and told him we were on our way but things were already moving so fast – he said they were already talking about the country going into 'lockdown'.

What the hell was that?! I started to hear that some other countries like China had begun stopping foreigners going into their counties and people were not allowed to go out. It all just seemed crazy! There was no way I would have ever believed that our government was actually going to make it law in the UK for you to stay in your house.

By the time we hit the tarmac in London, the wheels were already in motion. Constant news bulletins told us the nation was going into lockdown from the very next morning.

Rushing back to Hildenborough, we tried to work out when Kate could go back home. However, her parents being an elderly couple, they were unsure what to do and thought it best if she didn't return to the house. I had no clue it would end up being months!

My phone didn't stop pinging with messages from people asking if we got home alright; it was as if New York had become a war zone. I started getting emails from my PA Andrea who works for my company Double Gold Enterprises and arranges my diary and speaking engagements. The diary had been full of bookings for the spring and summer and suddenly they were cancelling left, right and centre.

The next morning I got up and went out to feed The Boys at 7am as I did every day. Outside seemed even quieter than usual, no distant sounds of cars trundling through the village, no trains and no planes, just dead silence. Back indoors the breakfast TV was showing pictures of central London looking completely deserted, without a single person on the streets. This was getting serious.

Anyone who knows me knows that when I'm stressed or when things seem to be going wrong, I have to keep busy. And with no work to do and the NYC trip cut short, there was nothing much else to do except exercise. I flicked through Instagram and psyched myself up to go outside and do a core workout. I saw more people than ever sharing what they were doing on their stories and grids. No one could go out, so suddenly everyone was online instead.

So one day, when I went out to feed The Boys, I filmed it and introduced each of them in turn to the camera. The comments went wild with everyone saying how cute they were and asking me questions about them. It seems no one had a clue I had six big fuzzy alpacas living out the back of my house.

Over the next few weeks they became celebrities in their own right: Polo, Liquorice, Toffee, Crème Caramel, Truffle and Fudge (who later passed away during lockdown and now his ashes are buried in that same field where his life with me began) with people messaging saying their kids were obsessed with them and wouldn't start homeschooling until they'd seen them in the morning. I got requests to see more of them and to watch them coming into my garden or getting a shower from the hosepipe. To be fair, it's pretty mesmerising because it's so weird!

A few days later I decided to go live and film myself doing my workout. I figured if they were coming online in the morning then perhaps I could encourage them to do some exercise with me too.

I'm sure some people thought I was mad at first just talking to myself and shouting into my iPhone as I counted through my reps but I was surprised to see quite a few people joining and making comments, cheering me on or saying how cool it was to see how an ex-elite athlete trains. It gave me a bit of a boost to be honest, whether they were doing the exercise or not, it was just about connecting with people through the doom and gloom. I decided to document my life through the weird times, not just to share it with my followers but to look back on it too. It felt like this was going to be one of those periods in your life you would not want to forget.

Each morning I filmed The Boys followed by my workout. Over the next couple of weeks, people watching my 'lives' went from a couple of hundred up to about three thousand at one stage, while I was doing my workouts. It was actually an amazing time. I was outside working out, the weather was incredible, the birds were singing like a choir. By now, Joe Wicks was doing YouTube workouts for kids, so I decided to do something a bit different.

I was getting so many questions about what type of training I did now I had retired and what were the best exercises to keep fit. I decided to go back to my PTI days and film some video classes people could follow.

Then, in one of my Instagram stories, I mentioned I would set up a live Zoom for anyone who wanted to join and I would send the entry code to anyone who DM'd asking for it. That evening, instead of going live on Instagram, I logged onto my computer and, one by one, little squares popped up on my screen. Some cameras were off so I said I needed them on as it would help me support them and correct any technique; I also didn't just want people perving and not participating!

Dressed in their sports gear all ready for a workout were all these strangers, young and old, men and women. I had no clue who anyone was and it wasn't my business to pry into their personal lives. I just wanted to connect. It was like my computer screen was a telescope into the living rooms, garages and gardens of all the people who'd been watching me but I had never seen, and now we could actually talk to one another. I went through the exercises and pushed them all to the end.

After one particularly successful session, I said I was going to treat myself to a gin and tonic. To my surprise, a lot of them stayed on and did the same and we all got chatting, getting to know each other. There were people from all over England, Scotland, Wales and Ireland, even France and South Africa, the place I call my second home. Andrea and a couple of friends I knew joined too, so it wasn't too weird and we all just had a laugh like we would have done with friends if the pubs were open.

Lockdown didn't turn out to be the couple of weeks we all thought, did it?! While the novelty of being stuck at home wore off pretty quickly for me, my fitness classes certainly didn't. As the community started to grow, I decided to call it 'Military In Motion', something I had started doing prior to lockdown actually, but at live health and fitness events.

One thing apart from running I think I am good at is being creative, so to switch things up, I started 'Nightcrawl' on a Friday night. My house became like an Amazon depot as each day I ordered wigs, outfits, accessories and props to make the workouts more fun and entertaining.

I figured we could all do with a bit of cheering up and the routines became more and more elaborate, with costume changes off-camera between songs, sometimes as many as eight times a night! Kate would be standing just out of view ready to whip me out of one outfit and into the next.

I think I ended up driving her crazy during those Fridays, repeating and perfecting every routine I was making up for that night. From John Travolta in *Saturday Night Fever* and *Grease*, Tina Turner strutting to *Proud Mary*, to the bearded lady from *the Greatest Showman* and so many more, I was shattered by the time I started at 7pm! Getting to know that community got me through the first lockdown when everything was so uncertain and the world felt like it was spinning out of control. Everyone was dealing with life changes in different ways and so was I.

In August, I was called in for an operation I had been waiting for. It was touch and go whether it would happen because like everyone, appointments were getting cancelled and hospitals were turning into Covid centres. I was extremely lucky to get my Haglund's sorted – a growth on the heel bone – because by now, with all the jumping up and down like a madwoman, it was killing.

Despite this physical setback I didn't stop taking the core in the mornings on Instagram even with my crutches. I adapted the sessions I was doing. Work started to come back and my public speaking engagements moved on to Zoom too. Do you know what? I actually started to really enjoy being at home for once. I missed Mum, of course, and it made me sad that I could only see my family on a screen, even 'celebrating' my 39 plus 11 birthday on my computer but looking at what was happening in hospitals and care homes up and down the country, I felt pretty lucky.

* * * * *

In October it hit me. Lying on the sofa, shivering, I pulled the blanket over me as my head was pounding. I didn't have a cough, but every breath felt like someone was punching me in the chest, it was so tight, and I just couldn't seem to catch my breath or fill my lungs with oxygen. After six months of lockdown and endless measures to try to stop the pandemic, Coronavirus had finally got a grip on the world and had got me! I felt horrendous.

I turned on the TV to see Boris Johnson standing there with his scientists again, peering over the wooden lectern with a very serious face. STAY AT HOME>>PROTECT THE NHS>>SAVE LIVES, the words screamed from a luminous yellow plaque in front of him. The lockdown had eased for a while but now we were back in the thick of it and I'd tested positive.

My temperature was through the roof and I hadn't slept properly for days as Covid-19 had taken over my body. I was in so much pain, I felt so weak and I could hardly walk around the house, let alone go out for fresh air. It had been a week since I'd seen those little red lines on the plastic test. I was getting worse, not better, and I was starting to panic.

"The number of admissions to hospital of people with coronavirus has increased again, I'm afraid to say," Boris told us as scary-looking graphs of the death toll flashed up on the screen.

"Next slide please," Chris Whitty, the man who seemed to have all the answers asked. "You will see this line shows deaths from Covid-19 in the last seven days," he said calmly. But the line on the screen showed a terrifying picture of the death toll from this mystery illness.

Just a few months earlier, life had been normal. I'd been travelling all over the world for work, speaking to rooms full of thousands of people, catching up with family and friends. But now as I lay there on the sofa in a cold sweat.

Now I was infected, I couldn't do anything, no Zooms, no workouts. Even worse, I was concerned because I'd had problems with asthma since I was a child, something I've always had to fight through in the army and during my professional athletics career. It was one of the reasons I'd always kept so fit and healthy through diet and exercise and generally caring for my body.

When we first heard about the virus, one of the things they said was that people who'd had underlying health conditions or lung conditions would have to be extra-vigilant because it could become very serious for them. Weirdly, though, we were finding out that really fit people were dying too – it was becoming crazy! Now I had the virus, there was nothing I could do except wait and hope it passed.

As the days went on, I lost all my taste and smell, plus my troubled breathing didn't seem to lift. There were times in the night when I was in so much pain, I worried I should go to hospital, but everything you read seemed to suggest you were safer at home.

For three weeks, I just battled through. As the physical symptoms didn't lift, Covid and being in isolation started to take its toll on my mental health too. Alone with my thoughts, I had nothing but time to relive things that still haunted me. I thought about Mum and how such a huge part of my heart still felt like it was missing. I knew you couldn't put a time on grief but at that point I felt no better than the day I found out she was gone, and wondered if I would ever feel normal again.

When I was rushing around working and seeing friends I could keep my mind off the dreadful feeling of loss some of the time but now I just wanted her there with me.

The worst thing was watching the TV and hearing about all the deaths, not just from Covid but because of other conditions that were not being treated during lockdown. It's no exaggeration to say there were moments when I thought, 'what if I don't make it through?" and started to think about my own mortality.

I imagined my friends and family being at my funeral, saying how sad they were for me because I'd never managed to truly find peace with myself and be proud of who I was inside. And what was there to stop someone going to the newspapers and telling them about my private life after I died?

It made me start thinking that it was MY right to talk about that part of my life.

I was honestly so low, I worked myself into tears so many times in those dark few weeks. It just made me so sad that I'd lost Mum and promised myself I would start living my truth on my own terms, yet here I was still a prisoner of my own silence.

Thankfully, after ten weeks, the physical symptoms of Covid started to improve. I finally got my taste and smell back and I began to build myself back up; at first just by walking as I was still recovering from my operation, and then gradually getting back into the gym. But while my physical strength was returning, I found myself firmly in the clutches of my spiralling mental health.

We now know that there was a huge spike in people suffering from anxiety, depression and other mental health problems during the pandemic. Perhaps it was the isolation, the uncertainty about the future and the time to reflect on the past or just sit with your demons, for me it was one of the darkest times of my life. That was when I realised just how bad things had become for me. Little did I know they were about to get worse.

After my previous breakdowns, I was no stranger to the feelings of helplessness and lack of control that go along with emotional and mental turmoil. But having promised myself on the day Mum died that would be the last time I would self-harm, my coping mechanisms, no matter how destructive, were no longer there as a crutch. I refused to resort to the bathroom scissors again or the relief I felt by piercing my skin and watching the blood flow. But my other coping mechanisms had all been robbed from me in the pandemic too.

You're probably getting the impression by now that I'm a 100-miles-an hour person. I need to be doing things all the time. I need goals and challenges and to be spinning plates in the air, that's how I've always been. That's just who I am – nothing by halves. It's probably the reason I managed to become an elite athlete while holding down a full-time job in the armed forces for such a long time, and how I'd managed to build a successful business, charity and public speaking career. I was rarely alone with my thoughts and when I was, that was when things started to go wrong for me. In the middle of the pandemic, with lockdown restrictions changing every few weeks, stopping us all from seeing our loved ones, working normally, travelling and doing all the things I usually relied on to keep me sane, I was lost.

Military In Motion felt like the only thing that kept me going. My 'Troopers' as I now called them, were amazing, sending me gifts and well wishes. I didn't let them know how bad things were for me, as I had only known them a relatively short amount of time. Yet they were my source of happiness and light during the days.

It was the nights that heightened my despair. As I felt myself plummet, I thought maybe I should try and get some professional help. It was clear now that this wasn't just something that happened when I was under immense pressure or in the shock and grief of loss, but something that was a part of who I am, and a result of my experiences over many years. I thought back to those little chocolate herbal tablets the doctor had given me all those years ago in France, the anti-depressants that my local doctor Paul had prescribed me during the years after retiring when I felt so lost and he diagnosed me with clinical depression. I didn't want tablets but wished I could see someone now. But the same fear was still there, holding me back. What if I went to see someone and they leaked it to the press, or worse, contacted the British Army to inform them? Would they have a duty to pass the information on if I had told them I'd broken the law? So irrational I know, but by now these were my deeprooted fears.

I should say for anyone reading this who has the same fears: doctors and counsellors are all bound by a code of practice which means they can not share your personal information with anyone else unless you give them permission. I should also say that you can't face court-martial for something which happened while you were serving the military as it is no longer 'a crime'. In fact it hadn't been since 2000 when the ban had been lifted.

I wish more than anything I just had the courage to compute this, because I would have saved myself years of anguish. But for over 30 years since I'd enrolled in the British Army, there I was, still terrified and ruled by those draconian, homophobic rules. I wished more than anything that Mother Dear was still around for me to talk to but she would never come back, plus she would have absolutely hated these times, it would have driven her crazy.

After my symptoms had eased and my fears of giving way to Covid had subsided, the feeling of weakness endured. I started going back into the gym, doing my workouts again, and getting the Military In Motion gang back together but off-camera I would feel completely drained. The same with work – I would get up and put on my make-up, choose a nice top, while keeping my PJs or leggings on under the table, trying to be all smiles and full of motivation for my audience for the hour they booked. Then I'd have to go for a lie down as I'd worn myself out. I just kept telling myself if I carried on eventually things would go back to normal. But once I felt physically fit again, something still wasn't right. That dark cloud of depression had got a grip on me again and I was really struggling to shake it off.

Perhaps this time I wouldn't, and that thought terrified me the most.

19

—

Rock Bottom

WHEN WINTER CAME AROUND, THE NIGHTS GOT
shorter and everything was dark and grey, it became even harder
to keep my head above water. When we first went into lockdown it
was incredible; beautiful sunshine, exercising outside, sunbathing
in the garden, but in the winter months it was pretty bleak.

Then one night I was lying in bed, unable to sleep when I
found myself completely hopeless. I still can't pinpoint what
exactly drove me to the brink but I began to envisage myself
creeping out of the bedroom and into the kitchen, and going
into the cutlery drawer where I kept the sharpest knives. I'd
promised myself I would never self-harm again, but this time
it wasn't a compulsion to cut myself to relieve the pressure and
jolt myself back to reality.

I knew it was more serious and, for the first time, I thought if
I had that knife in my hand, I could end my life. It's a terrifying
realisation for anyone to get to that point where you feel like
there is no other option, no way out of how you feel.

Lying in my bed that night I felt the muscles in my arms tense, pinning the duvet down either side of my shaking body as I stared into the darkness barely seeing through the tears. What was happening to me? Only months earlier I'd been petrified of dying from Covid and now I was imagining taking my own life. It made no sense.

The risk of asking for help now seemed somehow much less, when faced with the other alternative. It was as though the shock of thinking what I might be capable of jolted me into reality, just like self-harming once used to.

I reached for my phone and typed in 'celebrity psychologist'. It seems like such a weird search term doesn't it? I didn't type it in because I think of myself as a celeb! I did think if I spoke to someone who had experience of treating people in the public eye I could probably trust them. Maybe someone who made their living out of being discreet would be more invested in helping me keep my sexuality hidden.

The first thing that came up in my Google search was the psychologist who treated Jesy Nelson from Little Mix when she had her breakdown. I remembered a year earlier that she'd done a BBC documentary about her mental health struggles caused by the bullying on social media she suffered from being in the public eye.

Her situation was completely different from mine but we had a lot of the same symptoms in the end – feelings of hopelessness and wanting to just disappear from this planet. I thought if she'd managed to get help it was worth a try to see if this person could do something for me too, so I wrote an email, for the first time in my life, asking for help.

Even hitting 'send', I was terrified, but if it was a choice between that and slipping into a state where I wasn't strong enough to stop myself from opening that knife drawer, it had to be done. Even if it was 1.30am.

The rest of that night felt like an eternity until the sun came up and I forced myself to get out of bed, get dressed and log on for work. I still can't believe how I managed to keep going through such dark times but maybe it was years of practice. The same drive that made me cover my self-harm scars with make-up and get out there on the track or made me log on and give my all to the clients who had booked me to talk to their employees.

Since the start of the pandemic, all my speaking engagements and corporate training gigs had gone online just like everything else in the world it seemed. It was strange to have hundreds of faces in little boxes staring back at me or looking at myself in the screen, knowing they were all watching me with their screens turned off and volume muted, instead of standing on a stage and being able to see them all in the room with me; seeing their facial expressions, using my energy to inspire and motivate and feel that buzz and sense of accomplishment. But I had no choice if I wanted to keep my business going, just like so many other people who were adapting what they did to get by.

It's funny really, for someone who suffered so much anxiety and self-doubt in their personal life, but being on a stage transformed me into another person. It's like over the years I have become an expert at putting my game face on and doing the best job possible. Perhaps it goes back to my life as a PTI when I was calling the shots and shouting at groups of male and female soldiers in PT. Or perhaps it was just years of learning how to hide my true self that made me good at performing when I needed to.

Either way, usually I loved my job, meeting new people from all over the world in all different industries and sharing my experiences with them to help with their wellbeing and success. But now it was all online, just faces in boxes on a screen, it got harder as it wasn't the same. I still did my very best though, like running a race to get to the finish line, but when I logged off, I was back to feeling horrendous.

Thankfully, the same day I sent my email, the psychologist I'd contacted got back to me and suggested that we have a phone call to talk more about what I felt I needed and wanted from her help. I knew something had to change.

By now the world was burning anyway. Covid was showing no signs of stopping, civil unrest and global protests were sweeping the world after George Floyd's murder in the US earlier that year and it felt like there was no real hope of an end in sight.

So maybe now was time to just rip off the plaster and see what happened. We spoke on the phone for about an hour as I told her how I'd emailed in the early hours of the morning because I'd been worried about my mental health and frightened I might harm myself. I told her I'd lost Mum, that I'd had a history of self-harm and depression and that the global pandemic had brought it all to a head. Saying it all out loud actually helped in itself because it made me realise that actually it was no surprise that I was feeling this way when there was so much going on.

But there was that one big underlying secret that loomed like a shadow over everything else. 'F**k it', I thought, 'just say it'. And so I did. "I'm also gay but I don't feel like I can be open about it because I'm so scared!"

I had a few more sessions with her but it wasn't necessarily helping me decide what to do next. Instead of going any further with therapy at that point, I did what I knew best – I threw myself back into work and exercise. All my life, being busy and being successful have been the two things that have kept my head up, even in the darkest of times, and I thought if I could just keep my head above water like other people were trying to do during the pandemic, I would get through.

By now I was focused on another company I had started, creating a corporate health and wellbeing app with a guy who is no longer a friend after 14 years. I won't belittle him in my book but basically it showed a downside of mixing friendship with business. I was also running a lot of virtual medal events and challenges for Military In Motion and, apart from looking knackered, I am not sure they really knew what was going on. I wanted to keep them going as much as I could.

Logging onto another Zoom engagement one day in April 2021 I could feel my heart pounding. I felt like I was already on the verge of tears but I did what I always did – put a brave face on to get the job done.

On this particular day, I was asked to talk about mental health in the workplace. It was something that almost a decade after I first started championing it, was now becoming a bit of a buzzword in the corporate world. Talking about feelings and psychological wellbeing was no longer a taboo but something most businesses were having to do in order to stay competitive and keep their staff happy. There are awards for that sort of thing now and it has become a big PR tool for big corporations to prove they are doing the right thing and leaving the hard management and tough love of the past behind.

Usually I was well up for talking about it and I was always ecstatic that it was being taken more seriously and that people wanted to learn from what I had to say. But on this particular day, my own mental health was getting the better of me. I suppose there's kind of an irony there but as I sat in my office preparing for the call, I could feel the symptoms of self-doubt and I was procrastinating. Being cynical about my ability to do my job well. I was exhausted from not sleeping properly and my body was full of tension.

I felt sick to my stomach and shaky as I dialled into the call and tried my best to smile and put the Dame Kelly Holmes work face on. It's a good job it wasn't in person on a stage because it would have been more obvious how jittery I was.

But as I was introduced to the group by the session host, I just felt an overwhelming urge to be honest. It would have been so hypocritical of me to stand there and pretend I had it all figured out and had all the answers when in reality I was suffering right in that very moment.

"I'm here to talk about mental health," I started, wondering if they would be able to hear my wavering voice, "but I have to tell you, I'm not in a good place this morning. I'm really struggling."

I wondered as the words came out whether it was a huge mistake and I would be burning bridges with the company that had hired me to impart my wisdom to its staff, but I carried on and the more I talked, the more engaged the people looked. The more I spoke, and heard my own feelings out loud, the more I realised what I was going through and that something had to change. I had physical burnout.

That's the thing about poor mental health. First of all, it affects everyone in some way or another because we are all human. Secondly, it can hit you at any time. It's not like there is some magic cure or an off-switch. It doesn't matter how much success, money, love or time you have. It doesn't discriminate and doesn't stop you from ever suffering again.

That morning, I knew I needed to take a break. So as I shut my laptop, I knew that would be my last engagement for a while. Ironically, the feedback from the booker was amazing. They loved that I had been so raw and honest about the way I was feeling and given an insight to the people on the call about how mental health can affect even a Dame of the British Empire with two Olympic gold medals!

I texted Kerrie to tell her I needed to talk. She is amazing at that and I feel so blessed to have her in my life, even now after all these years. Just one message in the middle of a chaotic work or family time to tell her I need 'friends time' and she knows what to do. So the next day we met at Mum's bench.

"You have to take a break," Kerrie said as she looked at me and I told her about what had happened. "It's time to just focus on you for a while, you're completely burnt out and you won't get better until you stop."

I felt the tears pricking my eyes and I knew she was right. Here I was at 51 (ouch), with an amazing career, successful charity work, great friends and family but still the pain and fear of not being able to live authentically – to be who I am – was getting to my core.

As we sat on the bench I thought, 'what if Mother Dear could see me now?' She would hate how torn up I was over it all and that made it hurt even more. Back home that night I wrote a very hard post on Instagram and added a clip of me and Kerrie on Mum's bench. I wrote:

'Yesterday I met my amazing and lovely friend Kerrie, who has been my best friend since day one of secondary school (a long, long time). But she is someone who knows me so well, and knows everything about me!! (No, she won't tell). Anyway, we went to meet at my mum's bench and after a run we had a good chat… I think it's important to share. So this post announces that I will be stepping back from all my corporate and commercial work to

find 'me' at least until the end of May! Time out, doing jobs that have long been left, trying things that I haven't done, spending time with family and friends, setting myself physical challenges, doing my house and garden up, changing things that need to be changed, grabbing more me-time.

'This is one of the boldest, hardest, scariest decisions I have made since I retired from my athletics career (15 years ago). ACTUALLY I AM REALLY SCARED. But it's time and it's got to be done! I have had a few bad weeks of emotional dilemma and feel that I am not heading in the right direction. My mental health has deteriorated and I am scared I will regress to where I don't want to go. Whilst I am 'away' I will still be doing some stories but mainly about what I am doing, not necessarily about me. So, over and out on here for a little while.'

The two weeks I had in my head turned into ten months as I called off speaking engagements and other work to focus on getting myself better, but somehow things only got worse.

My mental health was at its lowest point during lockdown. During the 10 months that I took away from my commercial work, I was suffering both mentally and physically. My body was shutting down. My glands were up and I was getting cold sores on my face on a regular basis. When we were allowed out for exercise, I ran. In the past, running has brought me a sense of release and relaxation but now I was using it as a tool to punish myself.

One day I got out my weighted vest from my gym. The vest was 20kg! I put it on and ran down to Mum's bench. It's 4.5 miles each way, but I needed to get out. The constant narrative in my head was causing me to be consumed with the need to be free from my demons and, most of all, to be happy. Mum's bench became my place of solitude, as did the hills of Knole Park. My energy was so low after getting Covid, but I pushed myself so much. It was all just self-sabotage. I needed to get help. I was as scared as I had been all these years and yet the alternative of remaining silent and not using my voice was becoming more and more painful.

Because I couldn't speak publicly, I started recording voice notes on my phone. Maybe that seems silly as they were only for me to hear but I just had this overwhelming urge to use my voice and speak my truth even if I couldn't do it for all to hear. The notes became increasingly erratic as time went on and when I listen back to them now it makes me cry to hear just how desperate, trapped and helpless I felt.

"I need to use my voice, I need to speak up and finally be free to live as who I am. It's 2021 and I have kept this hidden for 33 years. I need to find a way."

* * * * *

I believe, if you let them, the right people come into your life at the right time and there is always a reason for it. Whether it was Sarah on that holiday in Chichester when I was feeling broken by my injuries or Pat on that beach in Cyprus when I needed my hair doing – or even the wonderful people brought into my life by Military In Motion thanks to the pandemic – I believe they all have reasons for being led into my world.

After my chat with my first therapist I realised that although I'd made the enormous step forward by asking for help, I hadn't quite found the right person and I couldn't let her in. A relationship with a therapist is a bit like a romantic relationship in that you have to have a certain chemistry for it to work; it's no criticism of anyone if you don't quite find the right match straight off. That was the case for me. I thought if I'd spent such a long time psyching myself up to tell someone my most personal problems and to try to get well again, I owed it to myself not to settle for the first person that came along. Then I struck absolute gold.

Dr Tania Pilley was not a therapist to the stars but there was something about her that just drew me in when I had the opportunity to speak with her on a Zoom. I felt instantly at ease with her. She was a straight woman about my age, who wore a pair of crazy multicoloured glasses on her smiley face.

She told me she used alternative methods as well as traditional talking therapies to help people achieve their goals, improve their mental health and wellbeing. I've always been the kind of person who prefers talking face-to-face so when Tania invited me down to see her in person to talk about things in more detail, I was nervous but felt positive. I got in the car and drove down from Kent to Dorset to meet at her home. When we saw one another, I knew almost instantly that we were going to hit it off.

We spoke for a couple of hours about what I had been going through and she asked me what had forced me to a crisis point when I decided to get help. I told her about the night when I almost relapsed into self-harm. She asked why I thought that was. I found myself talking more easily than I had done for years and gave her a brief overview of my personal story over recent years.

Tania diagnosed that I had childhood trauma, unresolved issues with Mum and with my time in the army, as well as the problem of keeping my sexuality out of the public eye. It was overwhelming to hear someone tell me all the things they feel might be causing so much pain but I felt seen and understood.

On my first day there, she suggested we do some work on my emotional state by doing Brainwave Therapy, or Neurofeedback as it's also known. I'd never heard of it before and it sounded a bit wacky but, to be honest, at that stage I was happy to try anything.

I felt strange sitting there in her little office at her house, with electrodes stuck to my head as she watched the brainwaves in my muddled mind. I imagined they would be going out of control with everything that had been swirling around in my head for months or even years but when she looked at the results, she just said: "You're flatlining."

I had no idea what she meant but she explained that I had become so exhausted and reached such a point dealing with my own stress and trauma that my mind had started to shut down on me to protect itself. She called this 'emotional flatlining'. The only time I'd ever heard the term flatlining before was watching medical shows on the telly and they never seemed to end well! But Tania assured me she could help.

I was only going to stay a night but that turned into almost a week. I talked to her about my earliest memories of Mum, St George's, and how I was terrified she would never come back. We talked about the feelings of fear and loneliness that came with realising I could have lost my career, and my failed relationships. And of course we talked about losing Mum.

It wasn't just the talking that helped, it was her mad personality and she made me laugh out loud, something I hadn't done in so many years. Tania was even delusional and insisted on coming on a run with me – let's just say, she never runs. I'm not sure she knew what she was letting herself in for but we had such a laugh, with her puffing and panting her way along the river banks, she said she thought she was having a heart attack!

Back at her house I found myself organising her kitchen cupboards and doing fridge management. We both found it funny that she was organising my brain and I was reorganising her kitchen.

At some point before the end of the week, after so much talking, we discussed what I thought I wanted from my life going forward and how I thought I could achieve it. It's such a big question for anyone to answer and in the past I never knew how to answer it, but I knew in my mind at that point that the only way I was going to be truly happy was to be honest about who I really am.

"I want to be free to be me," I said. I knew that meant one day I was going to have to come out and at last that felt OK.

20

I'm Coming Out

A FEW YEARS BEFORE I MET TANIA I'D MET A MAN called Emanuele Palladino at an event for British sporting heroes in London. By chance, I was seated on a table with him and his client, Welsh rugby legend Gareth Thomas. Gareth was equal parts inspiration and source of envy to me as he had bravely been one of the first international sports stars to come out.

In 2009, after his fourth Rugby World Cup, he became the first openly gay rugby player in the world. He then did an amazing documentary revealing that he was HIV positive and attacking the stigma attached to gay men in his position.

I have worked with a few different agents in the past including a wonderful lady, Bev James, who I had a close working relationship with, but sometimes it's just hard mixing friendship with business – although I am pretty sure our paths will cross again – and then others who I didn't feel comfortable being open with.

At the time, coming out seemed like a complete pipedream

that would never happen. I didn't even want to think about it. But after my breakthrough with Tania, I started to wonder whether I needed to get an agent who would at least understand some of the complexities around sexual orientation and 'coming out' so I emailed Emanuele and we arranged a meeting at The 1809 Hub, my former coffeehouse, Café 1809-turned-events space.

There we could talk openly about what I was going through. I explained to him that although many people had made assumptions about my sexuality, I had never felt able to live my life authentically in the public eye being a gay woman.

Sitting under the eaves of the Hub, with my victory pictures looking down on me, I discussed how I thought doing a documentary would be a step forward, enabling me to articulate some really sensitive subjects, whilst tackling the demons that I carried in my head; ultimately to move towards finally being true to myself and happy. I'd been on one tough journey, blighted by injuries and setbacks before fulfilling my dream as an Olympic champion, but an even harder one trying to fit within society, knowing that it would never be an easy task.

More and more I felt the need to publicly come out. I would swing between feeling desperate to do it and then being terrified. Growing up in the '80s there was a huge stigma around being 'gay' or 'bisexual' and I suppose I had seen over the years both the continued bigotry and judgement about people's sexuality if it didn't conform to the so-called 'society norm'. I also felt jealous of the relaxed way the younger generation were able to just come out with a single post on Instagram and then go on living their lives in a true and authentic way. I knew that could never work for me. My story was far more deeply rooted for that.

There was so much time that had elapsed since I first decided to keep my mouth shut about the people I loved that I felt I needed not only to come out, but also to explain why it had taken me so long. The last thing I wanted was for people in the LGBT+ community to think I was ashamed of being gay or that I thought there was something wrong with it. I needed people to understand that there was a very real and rational fear surrounding my silence.

The thing is, I actually don't think many people in society even knew a ban on being gay in the armed forces even existed. And definitely not that the European Court of Human Rights had ruled the ban on being LGB in the military to be unlawful in 2000 and that restrictions had been lifted. Also, in sport, how many world class gay athletes do you know that were out before 2004? Exactly?!

So, thinking again about Gareth and Jesy, I realised that maybe the only way to really deal with this was to tell my story in full by doing a documentary – a raw and honest look at what it was like to be me. And maybe then, as well as freeing myself from the burden, perhaps I would be able to help other people in the same position as me.

I had privately started to tell just a couple of people my idea and then Emanuele mentioned we could ask Gary Lineker's production company Goalhanger for a meeting about doing a documentary. I knew his company had produced some really hard-hitting programmes in the past so I had a feeling they might be interested, yet I knew there was one big hurdle if I wanted to even get them on board: I would have to actually tell them my story.

The idea of saying the words out loud still filled me with dread, but I was getting better at it, I had to keep telling myself that. If I wanted any hope of ever being able to go public, I knew I needed to be able to at least tell a producer. Plus, it wouldn't be the first time I'd been in a documentary, so I knew what to expect from the process to a degree and that helped keep me from completely losing it!

In 1996, as I trained for my first Olympic Games in Atlanta, USA, I'd taken part in a documentary narrated by Sean Bean, of all people. A film crew came to the barracks where I was still working as a PTI while training for the Games.

They filmed me putting a group of male recruits through their paces across an assault course, shouting orders as they scrambled over giant nets and ran around the field. I look back at that footage and smile at how strong and centred I seem doing the job I love.

It's strange to think that while I was excelling at work and in my sporting career, I was already hiding the secret that would come to haunt me so much in my later life. At that point I was just laser-focused on being a success, both in the military and as a runner. I was at the beginning of what would become an 18-year journey to finally getting my double gold and now I was at the start of another journey that I couldn't afford to take as long.

Luckily, my hopes of having a compassionate and trusting team around me were realised, when I met the Executive Producer Tony Pastor, Producer Jonathan Gill and Director Lucy Rogers. We met in the café of a big art gallery in central London. We had a discreet table in the corner of the room.

The place was buzzing with conversation and the clinking of cutlery and glasses. I still felt anxious when I had to say out loud: "I'm gay, I've just never felt able to say that publicly," but as soon as I'd said it, I felt more relaxed. It's such a strange feeling to tell people you're gay and get no reaction, when you've spent your whole life worrying about how people will respond. Of course it was brilliant to see how much the world has changed but it still blew my mind every time I said it out loud and no one flinched.

I spent an hour or so explaining to Lucy about the military ban on homosexuality and basically how I had lived a life of different traumas and the need to start to change that. Lucy and her team were astonished by my experiences and were keen from the get-go to tell my story in a documentary they planned to pitch to a TV channel. But before we could get the show commissioned, they needed to know if we could have access to the army of today; to interview serving soldiers and to go to the barracks where I could talk more about my life in the military.

It became clear from that first meeting that the only way to get my story out there would be to confront the very institution that had suppressed me and set me on a spiral of self-destruction, but one which I also loved and was still very much a part of since I was made Honorary Colonel. "I'm going to have to think about how I do this," I told them.

I also said that if we were going to work together, I needed to have full editorial control – this was finally my chance to tell the truth about my life and I wanted it to be in my own words, no one else's.

* * * * *

Back home in my office in Hildenborough, I started researching on the internet about what would happen to someone who came out as gay now, but had served in the army under the ban, but it just wasn't clear. Just like civilians didn't even seem to know the ban had ever existed, the consequences didn't seem to be discussed anywhere – perhaps because others in my position also felt too scared to speak up.

Instead I turned to Instagram and I came across the LBGT+ British Army Network page. As I scrolled through the pictures on their feed, I saw men and women proudly carrying rainbow flags while wearing their uniforms, and marching on parade at Pride events. There was even a picture of them laying a wreath at the Cenotaph on Remembrance Day and all of this was interspersed with photos of everything I love about the military – Queen Elizabeth, the stories of brave veterans, fallen heroes and shining medals.

I felt a pang of jealousy as well as happiness for the way things had moved on and they were allowed to live their lives so freely. It was almost incomprehensible how much things had progressed since I left in 1997. I knew the law had changed but I couldn't believe how open and positive the army now was about the very same people who just two decades earlier had been shunned, punished and ostracised. But most of the people smiling in the pictures were much younger than me and would have enrolled in the army long after the ban was lifted, so they were in the clear. I still didn't know what the consequences of coming out would be for someone in my position who broke the law of the time.

One woman who appeared to be central to the LGBT+ community was Colonel Clare Phillips, soon to be Brigadier. As a senior officer, and after reading a few of her posts, I guessed she was likely to have been in the army before the ban was lifted. Yet here she was still serving at a very high rank and openly celebrating all the diversity that makes up the forces now. For some reason I knew instantly, if I was going to tell someone once and for all, she was the one.

I kept turning over in my mind how she would react and how I would cope if she told me I could still be in some kind of serious trouble with the military. In my most paranoid moment, I envisaged the RMP knocking on my door and filling me with the same panic and terror they had when they raided our barracks rooms when I was 22! But what was worse – facing the consequences of what had happened 32 years earlier or living another 32 with it still hanging over my head? The truth was, I feared if I didn't do something radical I might not even be here to see the next ten.

I sent Colonel Phillips a message, but didn't tell her what I wanted to talk to her about, just that I was making a documentary and wondered if she could help me. She replied by giving me her phone number and organised a call to discuss more. Now there was no turning back.

As I waited nervously in my office for the time to tick around, I wondered whether I was making a huge mistake but I really was on a mission now. When I decide to do something in life, I don't stop until I get there, no matter how many hurdles I have to cross or how difficult it might be.

When she answered the phone, Clare sounded pleased to hear from me and addressed me with my military rank, as I did her, immediately making me feel that sense of belonging and pride that I'd loved so much during my time serving. I told her how I'd found her profile and explained I was planning to make a documentary about my life. Then I had to say those words again: "I'm gay and I was gay when I was in the army for nearly ten years but I have always kept it hidden because of the ban. If I come out now, what will happen to me?"

There was a brief pause on the line and then she said: "Nothing at all. Nothing will happen to you. The ban was lifted over 20 years ago and the army is a completely different place now." I should have felt a wave of relief wash over me, but to begin with I just couldn't quite take in the words. I asked the same question again and again, making sure she understood what I was saying and asking her if she was completely sure nothing could happen to me, but each time the answer came back the same – I was safe, I was free, no one could do anything to me now.

"I'm actually horrified that you thought you could still be punished now after all these years," Clare said. "I had no idea there were still people living with that fear, it must have been so difficult for you."

I felt my eyes well up as she told me she had also been forced to live two separate lives when she joined the army in 1995, and how she suffered many of the same fears and anxieties that I had.

We talked about the raids and the RMP investigations, hidden relationships and derogatory nicknames; all the things I'd buried in my past. It felt so good to talk to someone who had been through the same thing as I had, and to see that she's not only survived beyond the ban but that her career had thrived.

She told me that just a year earlier in 2020 she'd been invited to join the LGBT+ Network as a Co-Chair. She explained how the network aims to support army soldiers and officers who are members of the LGBT+ community and the army's chain of command. They even had equivalent networks in the RAF, Royal Navy, civil service and across the MOD, which blew my mind. It seemed it wasn't all just PR spin, the institution really had changed.

I knew if I wanted to tell my story, to really explain what had happened to me and so many others, I needed to gain access to serving personnel of all different ranks; to talk to them about their experiences – as well as people like me who had served in the bad old days under the ban. Colonel Phillips couldn't give me permission to do this, it had to come right from the top, Major General Neil Sexton.

I now had the assurance that I wasn't putting myself at risk of legal action or public shaming. My confidence was growing so I requested a meeting with him. The date came through for a Zoom meeting and this time as I logged on, I felt a sense of strength. I knew it was going to be much harder talking to a high-ranking, straight, white male officer who had served during the time when someone like me would have been vilified, but he had what I needed and I was determined to get it.

To my total surprise, as I started to explain the documentary, he seemed intrigued. I started to explain to him how frightened I had been throughout my adult life and that I could not take living in fear any more. I told him about the raids and the humiliation I had endured but also some of the deep mental health problems that it had led to.

He said he was sad to hear my story and ashamed of the way I'd been treated, but more so how it had affected my life. He told me he had no idea just how bad it had been for some serving soldiers who had endured this and even worse kinds of humiliation, but that he hoped it was much better in the military now and that he wanted to help me.

"You will have as much access as you need to the barracks, the serving personnel and anything else you need," he told me. "And after I'm gone from this role, I will make sure whoever comes next will allow you the same access until your story is told."

To hear him being so compassionate and supportive confirmed just how important my story was to tell. It was no longer just about me but about all the other loyal military servicemen and women who were victimised during their careers. A chance to speak for them too.

* * * * *

Three months after I decided to come out once and for all, at a meeting in a quiet bar at the Hilton Hotel in London Bridge, the dream became a very scary, but exciting reality. Emanuele and I met up with the Director of Sport, Niall Sloane, from ITV.

He listened to my wishes and all the access I'd managed to get from the army and he loved the idea. He commissioned a 45-minute one-off documentary to be aired on ITV1 later that year, the title being 'Kelly Holmes: Being Me.' It was my platform at last to tell the world who I really was. Not just a soldier, or an Olympian or a Dame but a proud gay woman who wanted to help other people just like me.

So that was it. I told my close friends and family what I planned to do and they were amazingly supportive. All any of them – Mum included – had wanted, was for me to be happy, safe and comfortable in my own skin and free to be me. As the filming got going, I asked Dad, Kevin, Stuart, Lisa and Kerrie, to come around when the filming crew were there. We all stood around the large kitchen island, reminiscing about when I first came out to them. I asked Dad for the first time how he had really felt when I sent him that letter from trade training to tell him I was gay.

"I just thought if she's happy enough then why not? It don't bother me!"

He's a man of few words in his best common Kent accent, but sometimes they are just the right ones! Hearing him say that again all those years later made me well up, as I had when he'd

237

called asking to come to the barracks and see me. I realised how lucky I was to have my loving family and friends around, who have always supported me and I also realised my story could have gone a very different way, especially knowing how dev-astating it can be for many of the LGBT+ community who get rejected by their families.

During filming I decided to talk to a couple of veterans who had been kicked out of the military. I went down to Bour-nemouth to meet a lady called Emma Riley who'd joined the Royal Women's Naval Service in 1990 to follow her dream of a military career. She told me that even though she was celibate, she was reported to the Navy's Special Investigation Branch just for telling someone she thought she might be gay.

"I thought she was a friend so I confided in her how I was feeling and then the next morning at 6am I was woken up and told to get up, get dressed, get downstairs, you're under arrest."

The 'friend' Emma had confided in had called the police to report her for even thinking she might be gay, let alone having a relationship with anyone. It showed just how deeply ingrained homophobia was in the culture of the military and it made me so sad to hear that she'd lost everything, her job, her future prospects because of it.

It was hard not to imagine how easily I could have been in that same situation myself if someone had chosen to dob me in, the same way Emma was betrayed and I started to feel my anger grow. I must highlight here that Emma has now become a good friend and we have been on a tough, but rewarding journey together since we met.

Another veteran I met, David Kelsey, who later became Mayor of Bournemouth, had been 'discharged with dishonour', marched out of his barracks and forced to leave his medal behind when he left. These people were willing to put their lives on the line for Crown and Country and yet they were treated like animals when they were found out simply for liking someone.

As a complete contrast, when I went back to barracks to talk to serving personnel about life in the army now, I finally got to meet with Clare, now Brigadier Phillips (for those that don't know about rank, a brigadier is a high-ranking officer). Anyway, for those who watch my documentary, you will see the huge sense of connection and gratitude I have for her. Speaking to the soldiers was so surreal as the parallels of our journeys were worlds apart, but it was heartwarming to know how much the world and the forces have moved forward.

I found it hard to get my head around how something so extreme could have really changed so much in the space of just a couple of decades, so I wanted to see it for myself. I knew from social media and the sporting community that there was one highly successful sporting couple who had been open about their same-sex relationship throughout their careers.

Lauren Price and Karriss Artingstall both won medals at the summer Olympic Games in Tokyo 2020 (taking place in 2021 due to the pandemic) for boxing but Karriss is also a former member of the Royal Horse Artillery, where she started her sporting career. The pair are openly gay and have supported each other to their huge successes which I think is incredible but so hard to comprehend how different life can be now for young sporting talent.

While filming, Lucy and I went to visit them in training at the English Institute of Sport in Sheffield and they seemed so happy and at ease with one another in front of the cameras as they spoke about their relationship and their careers. It was unimaginable to me just a few years ago that it could even be possible and I felt a twinge of sadness that I hadn't been allowed the same opportunities. It's easy to think about what would have happened if life had been different for me, but it wasn't, so I was intrigued to talk more.

To my surprise, Karriss never knew there had been a ban in the army and both of them were totally shocked to the point of welling up when I explained my journey. It is a very different experience for the sporting elite now. They come back from the Olympics and have the world at their feet, with social media deals and reality TV shows making them overnight celebrities.

I didn't have that same exposure in the early days but with what I had achieved, I do sometimes wonder what I could have done with that fame had I really embraced the opportunities that had come to me back then. The truth is I didn't know how to just be me and that was the biggest barrier I had.

* * * * *

As the release date for the documentary drew closer, I started to feel the fear and trepidation of the past coming back to haunt me and although I was excited at the prospect, the reality of the film going out to millions of viewers was pretty terrifying. Once it was out there, there was no taking it back, so it took all my strength to stick to my guns, not just for me but for all the other people I could be a voice for.

In one moment of doubt I FaceTimed the wonderful and hilarious Alan Carr, who I had met through world-renowned interior designer Kelly Hoppen, someone who had become a friend over the years and had invited me to her CBE celebration party in London. I had seen Alan perform in Belfast too and that was where I had originally told him about my doc.

So, back home sitting on my sofa, I explained I was finally

doing it, and filming was under way but that I was still terrified about the reaction of the public and what they would think about me hiding the truth for so long.

"Listen, Kel, not everyone's going to like it and that don't matter. If they have a problem with it, they weren't worth having around in the first place," he said. "You have to do this now, it's time. And when you do, you will feel like a weight has lifted, I promise."

Alan had a similar story to mine in that lots of people assumed he was gay before he found the courage to come out. He told me it was 'the worst kept secret in Northampton' when he told his friends and family but said that, just like me, he had to say it in his own words and on his own terms in order to really feel that freedom. I knew when I came out some people would say, "oh, of course she's gay, we've known that all along," but that didn't matter because I would be owning it and that felt like the most empowering thing.

Soon, I didn't have any choice because the wheels were in motion. The date, June 26th, 2022, was written on my calendar and seared into my memory as the day the documentary would air and my 34-year journey to freedom would be over at last. Then, a few weeks before D-day, I got a call from Emanuele.

"I don't think you should wait for the documentary to come out, I think you should do just one big newspaper interview coming out, and then tell the full story in the documentary after that," he said. "You'll be able to raise awareness and it will drive interest in the programme, and get the viewing figures up, so as many people as possible would get to hear your story, directly from you"

But I'd psyched myself up for the 26th! I thought I had more time to prepare in my head and now there was the opportunity of a big sit down tell-all interview and photoshoot with the *Sunday Mirror* the week before that. Emanuele told me he knew the editor, Gemma Aldridge, and had worked with her on the story of Gareth Thomas revealing his HIV diagnosis. He promised me she would make sure the story was told in the right way and wouldn't print anything without my permission. I knew the press would pick up on the drama of it all as soon as the documentary hit TV screens anyway and I envisaged sensational headlines about 'Gay Dame Kelly' screaming from the front pages, which was the opposite of what I wanted. Instead I wanted to come out in my own words, on my own terms, before the documentary aired, so I agreed.

It was a surreal experience sitting in a hotel suite on London's South Bank with sun streaming through the window and telling a journalist the story they'd all wanted me to tell since my victory parade in 2004. It felt like I was doing the one thing I'd spent my life avoiding. Amy Sharpe was a lovely young female reporter who put me at ease but I still couldn't stop from crying as I relived the journey I'd been on. I told her everything from the dawn raids to the first kiss in the laundry room, the fears, the mental health battles and why now at the age of (you get the picture – yikes!) I was finally coming out.

The nerves were out of control and my mind was racing. Would the paper turn on me and ignore how I wanted it said, or twist my words to sell more papers? What if I was making a huge mistake? It wasn't so many years ago that mainstream media was openly homophobic, just like the army, using language that would make anyone wince now.

But it was a risk I had to take. It was time.

Gemma rang me as I was in the middle of Selfridges in London, just before they were going to print. She told me the headline they were planning was 'Dame Kelly: I'm Gay' and it stuck in my throat as I repeated it back to her. Of course that was what I was saying but it was so direct and I thought it reduced my story to something much less complex than it really was. It wasn't just that I was gay, it was that I had been a prisoner of other people's opinions about sexuality all my life; it was that I'd been frightened into silence and not had a voice for so long.

"That's what I think the headline should be," I said, when I explained how I felt. 'Dame Kelly: I'm Finally Free to be Me'. Just as promised, they changed it and put a rainbow-coloured strap line above it, saying: 'Olympic heroine comes out'.

Gemma sent me a copy of the front page and there it was, in black, white and rainbow colours

While I waited for the story to hit the website and social media that night, I played Emeli Sandé's song *Read All About It* at top volume on repeat, practically screaming along to the lyrics as I kept refreshing the *Mirror* website on my phone to see whether it had been published yet.

> *I wanna sing, I wanna shout,*
> *I wanna scream til the words dry out,*
> *So put it in all of the papers,*
> *I'm not afraid,*
> *They can read all about it,*
> *Read all about it…*

As I sang those words, that was exactly how I felt. I knew once the story hit the newsstands there was no going back. Everyone would know and my life would be changed forever: I was ready. But I never could have imagined just how big a change it would be.

The article went up online late on Saturday night and, within minutes, my phone started to blow up. First of all it was messages from my friends and family. They all said how proud they were of me, that the article came across really well, which made me feel reassured that I'd done the right thing.

I decided to try to get some sleep before the big day on Sunday but then things started to go really crazy as I was sucked into this whirlwind of attention. Every few minutes my phone was pinging with DMs from people I'd never heard of, congratulating me on coming out, telling me I was an inspiration and wishing me luck with my new life as an openly gay woman.

People were telling me about their own experiences of coming out – some young, some older like me. Many were out and proud but others were still living in the darkness of fear, unable to be honest about their sexuality. At first I read every one, and realised there were so many people in the same situation as I had been; crippled by fear and suffocated by what I thought other people would think. Well, now I knew what people thought – they thought it was great!

With each message that landed, I felt my nerves ease a little but I had no chance of sleeping that night and as more people read the article, the harder it was to keep up with the messages.

I put the front page and a link to the article on my Instagram stories with a soundtrack of the Emeli Sandé song that was playing in the background, and hundreds of people started replying to that too. As the nerves began to subside, I felt like I was going to explode with relief and pride and excitement for my new life.

That was when things went really mad. Athletes who had worked with me years before got in touch to say congratulations. Sally Gunnell, who was always a huge inspiration and a friend to me in our Team GB days was one of the first. I'd kept the secret from her for decades as she stood on the sidelines with cashew nuts and drinks for me to get me through my rounds in Athens.

I'd only told her a few weeks earlier when we were at the Queen's Platinum Jubilee, that I was working on the documentary because I didn't want her to find out in the press. But when she saw the front page for herself, she sent me the kindest message, saying how happy she was that I could finally be myself in public and wishing me all the luck in the world; one thing to put into perspective is to remind you that I had NEVER told anyone during my 12-year athletics career about my sexuality so this was a massive deal to me.

Other famous faces followed. The bubbly Davina McCall who had been on my podcast *Mental Health and Me*; Fearne Cotton was one of a handful of public figures I confided in and said she would help me tell my story on her amazing podcast *Happy Place* if and when I was ready; Gok Wan and Tessa Sanderson who were also at the Jubilee and of course, the wonderful Alan Carr. Ironically, I had been on a reality show the month before called 'Cooking With The Stars', not saying a word about my documentary but then Dr Ranj, Josie from *This Morning*, my fab chef Ronnie and the rest of the team all congratulated me. The list goes on – it was crazy and overwhelming the support I got.

Over the next 24 hours, I just kept waiting for the backlash, the trolls or the negative reaction that had hung over me like a threat for so many years. I expected cruel jibes and nasty names like I'd read about from other people in the public eye, but thankfully they never came.

21

Loose Women and a Man Named John

FOR THE FIRST FEW DAYS AFTER THE *SUNDAY MIRROR* article came out, I was shell-shocked to be honest. I had built up a lot of anxiety, thinking life was going to suddenly change, I felt like I'd thrown a grenade and then run and ducked for cover.

I couldn't bring myself to leave the house to begin with. Social media was one thing but I had no idea how people would react in person, so I told myself I would stay home until after the documentary aired.

There was a huge amount of interest from the media and the LGBT+ community, which was overwhelming. I had every TV show wanting me on their sofas and invitations to celebrity events I would never have even considered going to before starting to fill my inbox.

It was a media storm that wasn't going away, one that I could try to ignore, or embrace.

I'd come this far. I couldn't hide, so my first appearance was on the sofa of *This Morning* with Holly and Phil. I don't actually know how I got through that interview, I felt so much emotion running through my veins. The simultaneous build-up of anxiety and relief was overwhelming. I was shaking like a leaf; a mix of embarrassment and pride. It was a little too much and I took a while to contemplate what I had done after all these years.

Later that week I was asked to be a guest on *Loose Women*. This was my first real interaction with 'national treasure' Linda Robson who I had watched on the sitcom *Birds of a Feather*. I had been told how she is a real gossip, something I learned for myself later that night! She and the other ladies were so kind; more about 'Loose' later...

Earlier that week after the story dropped, someone approached my team from the British LBGT Awards asking if I could attend on the Friday night, as a special guest and to present an award. It was the kind of thing I never would have considered before because I had always purposefully avoided the 'scene'. I am not sure people realised that, for me, any association at all with the LGBT+ community had been like a spotlight picking me out in the middle of a dark concert. Basically I avoided at all costs for fear of the association. But now this was a chance to begin to embrace it.

Over the years, I have been to many events, places and countries for work. Sometimes I would have the opportunity to take a 'plus-one', to support or help with logistics and travel and so on, but because I wasn't 'out' I would always introduce people as my 'friend' or 'PA' – I was soon to learn that admitting this was a big mistake!

I bought a canary yellow dress by Ruedi Maguire for the night. It had a pleated skirt with a split up the thigh and cut-out panels at the waist. A proper showstopper. I had my hair and make-up done before making my way to a stunning venue called The Brewery. I was ready to go when I got a call from my partner, Louise (yes partner, how refreshing not to have to hide or lie – you have no idea?!).

She was due to fly over from Northern Ireland to join me but her flight was delayed. "Noooooo, what are you talking about, delayed?! I can't go by myself," I totally panicked and quickly wondered if it was too late to cancel because it was my first time EVER at an LBGT+ event, my first public outing since I came out and my first time appearing in public with Lou. Too many firsts on this occasion, so I was already a bag of nerves.

Little did I know, Lou was already all over it. She called Kathy, who I must mention here, has become a really close and loyal friend. I met her also through Military In Motion during lockdown when she asked if I needed help with the community and ever since we have helped each other out in work and personal situations. I know she will be a friend for life.

Anyway, by the time I arrived at the event, I had been assured by Lou that Kathy and Andrea were on their way. Andrea had been with me for eight years and I think she knew that out of all the times I needed her support through the years, this one was a must! "Don't panic, we will be there, and have already sorted the train to London. We can be with you until Lou arrives. It'll all be great. You can't pull out now. I've got your back," said Kathy. I was so relieved.

So, I went as planned. Cameras flashed as I arrived and when I look back at the pictures now, I see how much I embraced the attention and openness that I could now portray. I was taken into a room away from the event as I was a 'surprise' guest. Kathy and Andrea arrived and we waited for Lou but when the event started, I had to send Kathy to the table and told her to tell Linda she was a friend of mine.

Suddenly, fright struck me – shit, Linda! Remember I said I used to pretend my partners were my PA or friend? Well, that was OK when people didn't know about me, but now it was a different story. The last thing I wanted was for people to assume any woman I'm with is my girlfriend – especially mates! The panic set in and as soon as Lou arrived I sent her up to the room with Andrea. Yep, exactly as I thought, Linda had already introduced Kathy as my girlfriend – OMG – to not one, but two tables of people. Then proceeded to say to Lou, "I think I have some gossip to withdraw." Moral of the story… don't tell Linda anything!

The crowd roared when I went on stage to present the award and that was the first time I uttered it out loud: "Freedom is my voice."

I had a ball like I never could have done before. The room was filled with influential people from the LGBT+ community, impressive business leaders and even politicians. It was like this whole world opening up to me, celebrating the very thing I had been hiding from all my life. I'm not going to lie, though, it all felt a bit surreal, outside of my comfort zone and I was taken aback with thoughts of, 'how did I not know these events even existed?!'

The next day, 24 hours before the documentary aired on ITV, I'd hired out a screen at the Curzon Soho cinema for a private screening, and invited 50 of my closest friends and family. We served popcorn and cocktails and all watched '*Kelly Holmes: Being Me*' together. There wasn't a dry eye in the house as they all saw for the first time the journey I'd been on. I think some of them knew what I'd been through but had never seen or heard me talk out loud about it in so much detail and they were shocked and saddened by what I, and people like me, had to endure. But the overriding emotion seemed to be pride. I was proud of myself too, and we finished the evening by partying in Soho until the early hours. I let my hair down properly for the first time as 'me'; drinking shots, dancing with some of my school friends, new friends and even my Troopers. The night ended in a complete blur. As per usual I was poured into the back of a taxi home. Put it this way, I don't go out much, but when I do, it generally ends up messy!

* * * * *

Who would have thought I would ever be a loose woman?!

"We think you should be a Loose Woman," said Judi Love and Linda Robson when I saw them at the ITV rooftop party prior to appearing at Pride in 2022.

"I'd love that" I said, with an *I can do anything now* attitude. Before I knew it, I was having a meeting with *Loose Women* Editor Sally Shelford and Deputy Editor Yiljan Nevzat and Emanuele at Soho House White City, across from the ITV studios

The week after Pride, Lou and I went away for three weeks. To be honest, I needed to process the emotions that had built up over the past year, bad and good. The reaction and response I got from strangers as well as people who had known me for years was overwhelming. And that continued for weeks and weeks after the newspaper article and my doc came out.

Once again, I had thrust myself into the limelight, the media interest in me and my experiences hit another high. Now I wasn't only a Dame, an Olympic medallist and an honorary colonel but I was becoming, more and more, a voice for the LGBTQIA+ community and for mental health awareness.

It was uncomfortable in some ways because – I'm the first to say – I was not yet an expert about gay rights issues because I've shied away from that world all of my life. I have so much to learn. But there was no question, I had a story to tell and experiences to share, which I thought might be comforting to other people.

So I jumped at the chance to go for a meeting with ITV about joining the *Loose Women* panel, as a regular member of the team. I was equal parts terrified and excited.

Sitting there in the meeting, we had a discussion about what I could bring to the mix and what I would and wouldn't feel comfortable talking about. We agreed that it would be a good fit but I wanted to think about it because the idea of actually being open and opinionated and totally 'loose' about my thoughts and feelings in front of a studio audience and live on telly was daunting.

The whole concept of Loose was really out of my comfort zone as I've spent my entire life being super guarded and private around people who aren't in my inner circle. Speaking candidly about emotions and feelings or elements of my personal life doesn't come naturally to me. But I was also aware that it was a great opportunity to use a platform to give my opinions and raise awareness for things that matter to me.

Plus, as a mixed-race gay woman, I think representation and visibility is important and to have someone who looks like me, lived like me and struggled like me, on a mainstream TV show like Loose can only be good for people watching, who share some of those characteristics, and I hope I help them feel seen and heard.

I try not to have regrets but one of the things I do think is a shame is the number of opportunities I've felt I had to turn down because they might put me too much in the limelight, make me fair game for the press, or people, who have known me in the past, could potentially reveal my sexuality before I was ready. Now that I've come out on my own terms, that fear is gradually easing, and I'm learning to say yes to things instead of no. So, even though the idea of going on Loose was scary, I felt like I owed it to myself.

My first appearance was in September and I was fretting over what the subjects of the day might be and what I would have to think about but then something happened that blew everything out of the water.

The day before I was due to go on the show for the first time, I was on the red carpet for the *Daily Mirror* People's Pet Awards at the swanky Grosvenor Hotel in Mayfair, with cameras clicking everywhere. Judi Love from Loose was presenting and I spotted Linda there too. There had been murmurs from around lunchtime that something was wrong with our Queen and for me, like so many, it was a news none of us ever wanted to hear, with notifications buzzing on everyone's phones: The Queen had died.

I walked up to the top of the carpet, saw Linda, grabbed her and sobbed. I couldn't stop crying! Everyone around was in total shock and disbelief, there was a commotion as I think the organisers were not sure what to do next. I didn't know if the event was going to continue and felt bad walking into the function, make-up running down my cheeks. It felt really personal.

I'd met the Queen so many times and spoken to her on a personal level, as well as her family, and I felt a deep respect and admiration for her and everything she did for our country. Having pledged allegiance to the Crown and served Queen and Country for a decade of my life, having once been a driver in the army as she had and currently being an Honorary Colonel of the Royal Armoured Regiment she'd been my boss – effectively.

As head of the Commonwealth, to which I had won two golds and one silver medal in my athletics career at the Games and winning multiple medals flying the British flag, she had been a huge figure throughout both my career and life. I felt the loss as though she was a member of my own family and I think a lot of people felt that.

Through so many ups and downs over all those years, the Queen was our constant and our strength as a nation. She saw us through conflicts and economic crises and the pandemic, not to mention the tragedies she faced in her own personal life along the way, so to face the future without her felt daunting and incredibly sad to me. I was deeply privileged to speak on various news platforms about my fond memories of meeting the Queen.

Loose Women was cancelled the day after the Queen passed to make room in scheduling for rolling news and tributes to her from around the world. A week after she died, a special edition of the show was scheduled and the producers wanted me on the panel. In some ways, the fact I had so much insight into the royal family and such respect and knowledge of the Queen herself made my first appearance on Loose very fitting, as I knew I would be talking about something that mattered to me deeply.

At the start of the show, we played one of the Queen's favourite songs, *We'll Meet Again* by Dame Vera Lynn and already I was holding back the tears. Ruth Langford, who was presenting, had to pass me a tissue as they flashed pictures of me meeting with Her Majesty after Athens in 2004.

It was such an emotionally charged atmosphere and everyone on the panel and in the audience was in tears. Each of the panellists, Linda Robson, Brenda Edwards and Jane Moore, spoke about their individual experiences over the years; meeting the Queen and working with the royal family and it was a really special tribute which I feel very grateful and proud to have been a part of.

It was in the second half of that first show that the conversation became more personal, when we had a conversation about dealing with grief. Of course whenever someone as high profile and well-loved as the Queen passes away, it can become very triggering for people who have lost loved ones themselves and it can intensify the feelings of grief and loss.

We spoke about the pain, shock, anger and intense sadness that can cripple you in the wake of losing someone you love and it brought back all those feelings I'd had about Mum, which was incredibly difficult. The Queen was of course the head of state and monarch, and Commander in Chief of the Armed Forces but she was also a mum, a gran and a great gran, and I couldn't help thinking what her entire family must have been going through at that awful time.

Although it was out of my comfort zone, I'm so glad we spoke about that because the reaction to the show was huge and I think so many people were watching and going through their own issues with grief. Such major events in our life can act as a catalyst for change. It was a very personal loss of my own that would provide the trigger for me to take those first tentative steps towards a brave new life as the person I was always meant to be.

* * * * *

The second *Loose Women* show I did was for the Queen's funeral in September 2022, which was another hugely emotional day but once again I had so much to talk about because in the interim period I'd been one of the thousands of people who queued up to see the coffin lying in state at Westminster Hall in London.

I can't describe what it was that made me go but I was in Liverpool for the National Diversity Awards which was held in the incredible Anglican Cathedral. That night, I was the recipient of the Celebrity of the Year Award. I had a fantastic night partying with some wonderful people until the early hours, after days watching the incredible outpouring of emotion on live TV. I couldn't get away from the feeling of wanting to pay my respects.

The queue had been taking people up to 14 hours at one stage and I had been messaging my mate Kathy all day. "How long's the queue now?" I'd keep asking. "I really want to go." I was due to travel to Belfast in the morning but this feeling didn't go away throughout the awards.

At 22:39, I sent some voice messages: 'Wanna meet me in London and join the queue? I SO WANT TO GO!!!"

I amplified my voice through the messages. Then back in my hotel room after the event, I just couldn't sleep. I knew there were only a couple of days left for people to join The Queue and get their chance to say a final goodbye.

At 02:21 I messaged: 'Still want to go'. The next thing I got a message back. 'Me too, I cannot sleep'.

Kathy was awake as she had been tossing and turning because we had both been saying for days that if we didn't go it would be the biggest regret we would always have. I don't want to live with regrets, and she felt the same way.

The 'need' consumed my thoughts, so I booked the 10.30am train back to London. I arranged for Sarah, who was by now one of my most loyal friends since we split up back in 2002 to meet me at Charing Cross with some clothes appropriate for queueing a potential 16/18 hours by now. A quick change in the smelly loos and I was ready. Sarah went back home on the train, Kathy met me on the station concourse, and the next thing we were off on a train to London Bridge. We pretty much ran to the start because there had been whispers of them closing it. "NO WAY!"

We joined the back of what was to become the longest queue I will ever wait in. It started in Southwark Park, snaking up and down the lines of barriers. It turned out to be more than just a queue though.

I began talking to a wonderful guy, a former serviceman called John who, at 95 years old, was planning on walking the whole way too and told me a story of the time he was on parade as a young lad and had got a glimpse of the King; no, not our current King – King George VI! He was there with his daughter. We chatted to the loveliest people around us from all walks of life who later became our 'queue buddies'. We were given our wristbands, I did a quick interview for TV and we began our pilgrimage.

It took us along Bermondsey, China Wharf, up towards Tower Bridge, onto the Embankment, past Shakespeare's Globe Theatre, Millennium Bridge, Tate Modern, National Theatre and Royal Festival Hall.

Everyone in the queue was sharing food with each other

throughout the day, but by now we were gagging for something hot, so we bought chips with curry sauce, and Kathy and I started drinking gin which all went down a treat! We walked over to the other side of Westminster Bridge and back down on to Embankment.

Earlier that day, I had started a chain reaction as Kathy and I were also part way through a Military In Motion Press-Up Challenge that I had set up for my 'Troopers' that month. So, to keep ourselves occupied, we had started doing them back in Bermondsey. Each hour I would encourage more and more of the queue to join us and even managed to convince some policemen and women to join in along the whole route!

Passing the Palace of Westminster across the river, looking at all the flags at half-mast, we started feeling emotional as we were finally getting closer. The sun was setting by now, as we passed the Covid Memorial, and did another set of press-ups as the temperature had rapidly dropped.

Finally after nearly seven and half hours, the first-aiders came and said that they could take John ahead of the queue.

"No, it's OK" he said "I will stay with you all."

"No way, you need to get to the end now and you have been an inspiration to us all," we said, feeling relieved that finally he would get to pay his respects and get somewhere warm.

I gave him a huge hug and a kiss goodbye and, through the power of social media, someone who had been following my stories on Instagram had managed to capture him walking into Westminster. That was so heartwarming.

Then, over Lambeth Bridge, we did our final set of press-ups. We dumped off all the food we had for the scouts to send back down the line or for the foodbank.

In Victoria Gardens, I got mobbed by people wanting photos,

which in some way felt weird but in another felt like a shared, lived experience and everyone was happy being there together, even if complete strangers. We got changed in the Portaloos. Then we did another dump of all liquids and so on – Kathy has reminded me that I was not happy as I had to bin my new bottle of Michael Kors perfume and MAC make-up!

There was a mass of X-ray machines and security – at that point the mood changed and was totally sombre, and silent. We went up the stairs into Westminster Hall, and despite watching the live feed of the queue the days before, it was totally over-whelming; the sheer size, and how magnificent the building was, you could hear a pin drop with the silence.

The coffin looked so small on top of the catafalque. We paused momentarily as we were so moved by it all; we went down the right-hand side, giving each other space. When we got to the front of the catafalque, I bowed my head, and said 'thank you'. I walked on out in tears, but stopped at the door to look back. Kathy had remembered a volunteer telling us to look back before we left the hall as it would all happen so quickly, and what good advice that was.

Our queue buddies were all in tears when we got out and we just hugged and cried. It was an enjoyable, long day with such an emotional end. They were memories that last a lifetime and to share them with a mate was very special.

I had also worked for a couple of news channels on the day of the funeral, having been situated literally outside Westminster Abbey watching the incredible military procession march past with the Queen's coffin carried on the state carriage. Reliving that day and the gravitas of my experiences on *Loose Women* was another emotional show.

Those two shows were a baptism of fire for my journey on

Loose but in hindsight I'm really glad I did them; it made me realise what a lifeline the show can be for people going through difficult times and how I really can make a difference and a contribution. It's not all about telling your personal stories or airing your dirty laundry, or being controversial, it can be about compassion and making people feel less alone, and that's really important.

I've loved meeting the ladies who have been the stalwarts and backbone of the show and the newer panellists who come from different worlds to mine.

Meeting the different audiences, I've spoken openly about my complex life. My experience as a perimenopausal woman I hope has helped others in that position as the symptoms can be really confusing, hard to deal with and they're not spoken about enough. I have been given a platform to support the LGBT Veterans Campaign led by Lord Etherton, where we recently had the Prime Minister apologise in the House of Commons, for the mistreatment and unethical, historical ban on LGBT serving personnel.

I find it extremely hard to talk about my personal relation-ships – I mean, let's face it, you have read about them and this is the most I have ever said in this book, let alone saying it all on live TV!

The thing is, I still get anxious every time I go on the show because it is ingrained in me to worry about what people think and the judgement that I am open to by being on TV. But what matters is that I have been given an opportunity to grow and, as I write this, I am celebrating a year on the panel. I have been given new life experiences and, for that, I am truly grateful.

This is a new chapter of my life. Who knows how the story will unfold but what I do know is that I will take up as many opportunities as I can, especially on TV, as there's so much more I want to do. When people shout, "Are you ready?", I shout back, "Born ready!"

22

Love is Love

WHEN I WAS YOUNG I THOUGHT MY INDIVIDUALITY and differences from other people around me was a superpower. I hated the thought of being put in a box. In the army and then in the sporting world, I found my uniqueness comforting, until I found it a burden.

After I came out publicly as being gay, one thing I did find scary was finding my place in this wonderful, vibrant, new community that I suddenly found myself immersed in. The past 15 months since I first stood on that stage at Pride, has been one of the biggest learning curves of my life. I feel as though I have missed out and have half a century of catching up to do when it comes to learning about the LGBTQIA community. Before I went public, I never engaged with it, I actively distanced myself from anything to do with it in case it would blow my cover.

In some ways it feels amazing that I'm now surrounded by people who have shared experiences with me and who understand elements of what I've been through as well as the challenges that come with being gay and coming out. In others, I feel sad that a massive part of my life has been wasted, hasn't been as fruitful and definitely hasn't been as colourful or happy as I am now.

One thing that is really important to me is that I can learn about the community. Over the years I have seen the transition and growth within the community while watching from afar from what I knew growing up, LGB – 'Lesbian, Gay and Bisexual'. Out of all the letters in the acronym LGBTQIA, the 'L' was the first to come into existence.

For centuries, the word had been associated with the works of Sappho, an ancient Greek woman from the island of Lesbos who wrote poems about same-gender passion. The interesting thing is that I have always hated the word because, growing up in the army it always had derogatory connotations – you were called 'Lezzo' or 'Lezzer'. So I have always referred to myself as a gay woman (in my private life, of course). So who would have thought I would become friends with 'Head Lesbian' – as she's affectionately known within the community – Linda Riley, publisher of DIVA Magazine!

She befriended me backstage at Pride and we instantly hit it off. Linda has been instrumental in the community for years and has helped me navigate this colourful new world I now live in. I am not afraid to challenge some of her ideals, even to the point of saying I prefer to identify as a gay woman because that terminology sits far more comfortably with me, mainly because the word Lesbian was so derogatory in the past. But I have learnt it is each to their own and that's what acceptance is. She has introduced me to so many fantastic people who have taught me so much already, and I want to continue to learn.

I don't know how I feel about the idea of being some kind of gay icon, but I was very proud when I appeared on the front of DIVA magazine and have been so grateful to have appeared in so many LGBTQIA influencer lists.

I have also been lucky to win so many other awards in the short time since coming out. Including 2022 Hello! Inspiration Awards – Trailblazer of the Year, where I met the legendary Joan Collins! 2023 DIVA Media Personality of the Year and 2023 Rainbow Honours, Celebrity LGBTQIA Champion of the Year. What has been the most rewarding part of coming out, apart from being so happy, is that I can use my platform to be a voice for those who don't have one.

Just like I wanted to help underprivileged young people through my charity The Dame Kelly Holmes Trust after my Olympic success, I am using my voice to amplify the messages around the importance of psychological safety, equal rights and the need for people to feel heard. To connect people and be instrumental in the fight against any bigotry and discrimination. I used to laugh at the extension of the community 'alphabet', not understanding the need for so many letters, until I realised it's important to have a sense of belonging. It's been an emotional journey of exploration for me as I find my feet in my 'new' world, but I am loving the freedom it gives me too.

Perhaps the most important thing for me, though, has been my involvement in Lord Etherton's review into the treatment of LGBT veterans. He chaired the review to try to settle once and for all what really happened to the thousands of men and women who were persecuted in the military because of their sexuality, and to make amends.

After *Being Me* aired and he saw the people I'd spoken to in the making of it, he was keen to get me involved, and I wanted to help in any way I could. The problem they had was that they were struggling for people to come forward and give their testimonies, so I decided to use my platform to try to get people to contact the review team. I did interviews in the press, shouted about it on *Loose Women* and posted on my social media to try to get people to get in touch, and they did, in their hundreds.

A few months ago we achieved the most amazing victory for thousands of veterans, including myself. Prime Minister Rishi Sunak gave an apology in Parliament, for the way that LGBT veterans were treated, not only during their time serving their country but also because of the long-term damage it caused so many of us after we left. Hence my deeply-engrained fear of coming out.

The Government read the report from Lord Etherton's review, which has 49 recommendations for 'righting the wrong'. We got to go to the House of Commons to listen to former Secretary of State for Defence the Rt Hon Ben Wallace MP give his passionate statement following the publication of the Independent Review into the service and experience of LGBT veterans who served prior to 2000. Basically the mistreatment and injustice suffered at the hands of a barbaric ruling and law – and this was acknowledgement at last that the way we were treated was wrong.

It was such an emotional but rewarding day. The recommendations in the review will make real change in the armed forces and hopefully mean that all veterans can now be proud of serving and start to rebuild their lives.

I was invited with other veterans to represent more than a thousand brave men and women who submitted testimonies of our experiences in which between us we were arrested, raided, interrogated, dismissed, bullied, sexually abused and jailed. In some cases, losing the right to a career they loved, having medals stripped, pensions taken away and, for everyone, mental health trauma

The charity, Fighting for Pride, and Emma Riley from my documentary were instrumental in campaigning along with other charities and individuals like myself, *Loose Women* and the *Sunday Mirror* who also supported the campaign. Being there when LGBT+ veterans were heard and cared about in Westminster was such a momentous occasion for me and for everyone involved.

A couple of years ago, when I was on my journey to freedom, I decided I wanted to mark that in some official way. Not many people know this but 'Unique' isn't just something I use as a mantra, it's actually officially now part of my identity – legally!

Having spent years hiding parts of myself but also struggling with my identity in some ways, I decided to change my name by deed poll to have 'Unique' as a middle name. I might sound absolutely nuts, but during lockdown when I felt like I was 'losing the plot', I'd thought about changing my name many times.

I considered many times over the years about changing Holmes to Dad's name Norris and to distance myself from the 'sperm donor' but everyone who knows me and has supported and celebrated my achievements over the years knows me as Dame Kelly Holmes, so it would seem strange to change that now. But adding middle names to my legal title seemed like a great way to be reborn in a way as a new me and to celebrate all the different and wonderful things about my life and my identity.

I have carried the name 'Unique' with me most of my life, as a protective shield, and now as a celebration of everything I am. So when I got the form from the deed poll office, I didn't hesitate to fill it in.

The second name I chose because it's just as special to me. When I lived in South Africa there were beautiful birds of paradise; they were so bright, colourful, and resilient. The native birds also symbolise freedom and the bird-of-paradise plant which looks just like the bird itself, with bright yellow flowers and beautiful blooms, was named in honour of Nelson Mandela's long fight for freedom during the Apartheid era.

So my name now is Kelly Unique Paradise Holmes. Some people may think I am strange, different, mad but guess what? I LOVE ME! And you never know, I may need a stage name one day – ha!

* * * * *

Standing in the pouring rain, looking out over a misty-grey cove on the west coast of Ireland, with the wind whipping around the hood of my poncho, I couldn't believe it was the middle of bloody August. But while the weather was a total disaster and I had no idea where I was going to sleep for the night, I wouldn't have been anywhere else in the world if you'd paid me. I guess that's how you know you really love someone – when the only thing that matters is being with them.

Of course, a tropical island in the blazing sunshine would have been nice, but since I have been seeing Lou, I knew I was in for a few trips to the Emerald Isle instead and, to be honest, I was all-in. She's an Irish lass through and through, so it comes with the territory: rain!

People who follow me on social media have probably seen Lou's face pop up more and more over the past year, but we've never gone 'Insta-official' and I deliberated long and hard over whether to talk about my relationship in this book. Yes, relationship! I don't want to go all soft and, as you know, it takes a lot for me to talk about personal relationships, but finally, after decades of failed flings, relationships that have not been successful and a life that has been lonely at times, I've found someone to share my world with, and I'm happier than I have been for a long time.

I'm not going to say too much about Lou here because if she ever wants to talk about being in a relationship with a runner-turned-Dame and telly presenter, that will be her story to tell. But I couldn't let this book come out without acknowledging how happy I am to have her in my life right now.

It's true what they say that it's when you're least looking for someone that they can just walk into your life. In the depths of lockdown when we were in a global crisis and I was still grieving for Mum while trying desperately to hold things together, Lou was one of the many amazing people who joined Military In Motion, my little fitness community that became my lifeline.

We didn't even meet one another for over a year because we were in lockdown and we hardly chatted in the group as there were people much louder and more prominent than she was.

When lockdown restrictions started to ease, I met up with my wonderful 'Troopers'. Even the first few times we met, Lou and I rarely spoke to each other: she was in a relationship and she never bloody spoke to me anyway! Maybe because I was 'Troop Leader' but she now says it's because she was shy!

Over the following few months, the community as a whole kept getting stronger and closer. Even though we both had people that were part of our lives during lockdown, I think our stars aligned.

It was after we met again as a smaller group that I got to know her more. I personally think things happen for a reason. Lou's relationship broke down and gradually, over time, we seemed to connect more and more and here we are now.

She lives in Northern Ireland and our lives couldn't be more different but she's kind and trustworthy and we have so much in common. She's got the fitness bug too and we love running, hiking, paddle boarding and generally getting out in the great outdoors together and having fun – with a few gins and cocktails thrown in for good measure, of course.

For the first time in years I feel totally comfortable and have no doubts about her wanting to be with me for my achievements or my titles; she just loves me for me, the mad, crazy, frantic, workaholic me, and that feels great.

After the enormity of 'coming out' and going to Pride, I went on holiday for three weeks with Lou. There was a lot of emotion, both cheers and tears, so I needed to get some headspace.

Feeling liberated, Lou and I visited San Francisco's Castro District, commonly referred to as The Castro, in Eureka Valley. The Castro was one of the first gay neighbourhoods in the United States and boasts an iconic giant flagpole and oversized rainbow flag as a proud symbol of the LGBT community.

We did one of those free audio tours and walked about the streets, passing the lively bars like Moby Dicks, taking pictures amongst all the colour and vibrancy. I was fascinated by the story of Harvey Milk who was an American politician and the first openly gay man to be elected to public office in California. It was his strength of standing up for others that paved the way for LGBT movements across the world. I would NEVER have gone to a gay area on holiday before, so whilst it was a bit scary, it also felt awesome to be free.

I won't go on about our relationship any more, because I've realised that it's our story, and hopefully one to elaborate on another time. But we are enjoying life between sunny Kent and rainy Northern Ireland, and I hope we have many happy years together ahead of us. Only the future will tell what happens next but I'm incredibly grateful that we met.

Love really is love, no matter who it's between, and there is so much worry and stress in the world, we have to make the most of the good times when they come our way and celebrate love where we find it – even if it's in the least-expected places.

It's taken me a long time to realise that there are many different kinds of love in the world and, throughout my life I've been lucky enough to experience many of them: The love of my best mates Kerrie and Sarah who have stuck by me through thick and thin and who know me better than anyone. My home and school friends who have only ever known me as just Kel. The love of the siblings I grew up with – and the ones I missed out on as a child but have grown to feel they were always part of my life. My wonderful nieces and nephews, who I hope will always understand acceptance. The love of my loyal dogs and, of course, The Boys.

I've had a first love. The love of my dad, who took me on as his own from the day he met my mum. Then, of course, Mother Dear. I still miss her every day and I'm forever grateful for how losing her started me on my five-year journey to being free to be me. I wish she'd lived to see me so happy being free, but I believe she's around. I still see the odd butterfly, a white horse or feather to remind me she's here.

Then there's been the love of the British people and sports fans around the world that I felt so strongly when I won my two Olympic gold medals – for them – and finally, the new friendships I have made who have come into my life in recent months and who have embraced the 'new' me. I LOVE YOU ALL.

I'm sure there's plenty more love in the world, for me and for you. Our lives are made up of different pieces of a puzzle and love should be one piece that's in place. It should not matter where it comes from or who it's with, whether you're straight, gay, trans, bisexual, black, white, rich, poor, big, small or anyone who fits within the glistening spectrum of light that comes from a diamond. Everyone deserves love and to live without fear or judgement, every love deserves the same respect. It's what gets you through the darkness and makes the highs of your life so much higher. Having love and acceptance is a safety net and a comfort and brings so much joy, so let's embrace it. Love is love. And remember, every love is UNIQUE.

I want to leave you with a few words from a song that I heard that makes me feel proud and for anyone else who needs strength, you might like it too:

Wyn Starks

I've been closing the door
All my life, held it in but not anymore,
Got two feet on the floor,
This is it, I'm stronger than before,
Pardon my imposition,
But this is my conviction,
I need to get this off my mind.

I gotta be me, gotta be I
Gotta be who I know I am inside
Can finally breathe, taking it in,
Look at me flying!
It's always been there,

LOVE IS LOVE

It just took me a minute to find it,
If I were to be anybody else,
I'd just be hiding
Who I am
Who I am

23

Life Update

THIS YEAR IS MASSIVE! IT'S ONLY THREE MONTHS until my Olympic games' anniversary and I've found myself boarding the plane back to the birthplace of the first modern Olympics held in 1896, Athens. I am excited to explore the city where I first realised my athletic dreams all those years ago because as an athlete you never really get to see the country you compete in. It's been 20 years since I won those elusive gold medals at the Athens Olympic Games. Life has changed for the better. I feel empowered, energised and motivated; stronger in my mind than ever before. I am ready for my next chapter and all it will bring.

This chapter starts with imposter syndrome. Heard of it? Well, it's defined as 'a person who doesn't feel confident or competent, regardless of what they achieved'. Never in a million years did I think this was me until this year and it has hit me hard.

On *Loose Women*, I have had moments of paralysis, anxiety, and procrastination as a result of imposter syndrome. Not because of other panellists, but because of my own insecurities and hangovers from my past. The nature of the programme exposes you to criticism and always makes me wonder if I'm doing okay. I find I'm always self-conscious and worrying about embarrassing myself when I'm working.

So, how did I resolve this? I spoke to a couple of the other *Loose Women* panellists about these feelings and was surprised when they responded saying they had felt the same way. I hated the thought of feeling needy but at the same time I needed validation and positive feedback. Knowing I wasn't the only one put me at immediate ease. Having that 'phew, it's not just me' moment was a relief and that's why in all situations, conversation is worthy and powerful because you are never alone in your insecurities, there is always someone else going through the same thing.

On reflection, I've realised it's the inherent drive for perfectionism and people-pleasing I have that makes me this way. I hate not feeling good enough or thinking others may think I'm not good enough, but I also hate not being in control of those feelings and internalising too much.

For me, the intense determination and focus that stems from being an athlete means I always want to know if I am doing well. In sport this is very objective; you win or you lose, you get better or plateau, you are 'great' or just not very good anymore. The thing is you know where you stand and how to get better so it's easy to evaluate your achievements. That's why, despite it being so challenging, in sport I always knew where I stood and that's where my self-confidence came from. But I am no longer an athlete and the rest of the world doesn't measure success with medals or rankings.

Can you believe it was a stint on the boards of the Theatre Royal Plymouth that lifted every inhibition I have ever had and cured my imposter syndrome? Plymouth, a port city in

Devon, southwest England, known for its maritime heritage and historic Barbican district with narrow, cobbled streets. A city I would find myself inhabiting for almost five weeks after somewhat hesitantly agreeing to perform in a pantomime down there.

I say hesitantly, even though I technically manifested my appearance. First, let me tell you how this came about. It was a moment of madness that has pretty much shaped how I feel and act today.

Award winning singer, songwriter, actress and radio personality, Beverley Knight and her lovely husband James had invited Lou and I to the opening of May Fair Kitchen, a wonderful restaurant on Stratton Street. Kara Smith, a freelance PR and talent booker, (someone who has since become a close colleague) and her DJ husband Munro were also there as we rubbed shoulders with my Olympic buddy Denise Lewis, comedian and actress Chizzy Akudolu, *X-Factor* runner up Rhydian, and award-winning actress, singer, and dancer Cassidy Janson. (She previously played Anne Hathaway in the West End production of *& Juliet* another musical theatre production I adored!) There I was introduced to Jason Manford, the multi-award-winning stand-up comedian, presenter, actor and singer, who turned up a bit late after a performance.

Fast forward a week and I am now watching Jason (who I had been bugging about tickets) playing the Cowardly Lion in *Wizard of Oz*, the musical based on the iconic story by L. Frank Baum, which was playing a limited run at The London Palladium in the summer of 2023.

After the performance I was chatting with Jason and he asked me, "Would you ever do theatre?" I'm not sure if he could sense my internal horror at the thought of standing up on stage in a large theatre, all eyes of the audience fixed on my appearance and judging my performance! After less than five seconds, I said, "NO WAY!"

Later I found myself standing at the top of the stairs in the bar of The London Palladium with Kara and Munro, gushing about how brave Diversity's Ashley Banjo was in his first musical theatre production when Matt Slack, a friend of theirs from Birmingham who writes panto, came over to talk to us. I perked up and jokingly told him, "Ooh, maybe I could do panto." Why did I say that? At first, Kara asked if I was being serious, to which I said, "Yes", and Matt instantly proclaimed that he would write me into one. I thought nothing more of it and moved onto the numerous press photos being taken that night.

Fast forward four months and I'm running from London Bridge train station at 9:20am in the December rain. I hold my coat over my hair so I'm not turning up to my 'first day of school' looking like a drowned rat. I sprint towards The Jerwood Space Studios on Union Street London where I was going to spend the next six days rehearsing for my role as Ringmistress Olympia in the panto production of *Goldilocks and the Three Bears*. You might be thinking, 'How on earth does a ringmistress fit into that story?' I asked the same question until I realised that the script was set in a circus, which raised even more questions! 'What the hell is this all about and what on earth am I doing here!?' I thought. I was about to find out how tough this theatre world really was.

Now, for those that don't know, the pantomime is steeped in British history and was first developed in England. It's a musi-cal-comedy stage production designed for family entertain-ment. Pantos are performed throughout the United Kingdom,

Ireland and other English-speaking countries, especially during Christmas and New Year.

My role had come about when I told my manager my mad idea of doing panto. He contacted someone he knew called Jonathan Kiley, a casting director for Crossroads pantomimes and 'an old queen' of the theatre world. Jonathan would go on to remind me of my army days. A casting director is a lot like having a sergeant major: very strict and always bellowing out orders.

It was a last-minute deal, but Johnathan was keen to explore where he could fit me into the show. I did 'um' and 'ah' over it for a while, considering all the work I would lose out on while committing to this role: speaking engagements, Christmas parties, and the general disruption it would cause. Lou had just moved over to England from Ireland and I would now have to tell her we would be living in Plymouth for five weeks. All in all, I'm not sure how well I had thought this through, but I had opened my mouth now and I hadn't a clue what I let myself in for!

First, I realised I was with seasoned performers who knew everything about scripts, how to act, dance and sing, even if that wasn't their primary skill. They could do it all. We stood around in a circle in a large studio with mirrors all on one side and introduced ourselves.

I had met some of my castmates, including former *Strictly* pro dancer Brendan Cole, comedians Samuel Holmes and Adam Booth, ventriloquist Steve Hewlett, Corrie's Alexandra Mardell and Jonathan at a press event a month or so before. There was now the wider team who were running the shows.

Rehearsals began and we each had our scripts and I could see that some had highlighted their 'parts'. To be quite honest, I had that book for about 10 days and I had looked at it twice. Mainly because I was so damn busy being 'Dame Kelly' and foolishly assumed I didn't have much to say when I briefly scanned the sheets.

It wasn't until I was stood there in Jerwood Studios for the first rehearsal that I realised I had to read this long tongue twister of a monologue…

"People of Plymouth, please welcome, with his audacious amalgamation of agility and equilibrium, his peerless pageantry and imperturbable pluck, a scintillating spectacle of juggling japery, the likes of which has seldom been prognosticated, let alone accomplished, all the way from Mexico, the one, the only, El Mariachi Marquez!'

'No way can I remember this,' I thought. There was also a scene titled: *"IF WE WERE NOT IN THE BIG TOP" – OLYMPIA (Pancake chef with frying pan)*

"Flipping here, flipping there, flipping pancakes everywhere"

Honestly, I thought I was saying a poem. Little did I know I was going to be part of a traditional 'pantomime montage' that would span five whole minutes – shit! What am I doing? Can I get out of this whole process? Shall I admit defeat and say I had made a mistake? Before I knew it the week was over and I was still very much in the show, despite spending every night dreading the next rehearsal.

The six long days of rehearsals went by in a flash and on Sunday Lou and I packed the car up to the brim with Shiloh (the dog) in tow and set off to 'our new home', a cute two bed apartment situated 30 seconds' jog from the theatre and a five minute walk to the Hoe.

I am not sure how many of you reading this know what Panto is or have ever seen one so I'll try not to make the next five pages all about it, but I do need to explain what happened to me during this period of time and why I have come into 2024 with this newfound confidence and have hit the 'fuck it switch'. I don't care what people think anymore and it's incredibly liberating!

After the an intense daily eight hour rehearsal for four and half days at T2 – a much bigger rehearsal building – we were preparing for our first live show in the Theatre Royal. I had dressing room number two with my name on it and three sequined outfits with hats, gloves, boots, whips and a wig ready and waiting. Then the panic set in. I had to do my own make-up for the whole show – every show – and let's remember I was not cast as the pantomime Dame! So I just came up with a look for each outfit knowing the audience would never get that close for me to worry about how much I had plastered the eye shadows and foundation on. I even dared to have dark red lips, not something I feel I pull off that well, but I went with it.

There I was on stage dressed in sequins, acting stupid, trying to regurgitate the words that had now been ingrained in my head for fear of looking like a right fool. Did I forget some? Of course! Did I feel nervous every show, twice a day, six days a week? Yes! Did I mess up? Oh, yes I did! Did my wig come off mid-scene for me to completely adlib "my wig has been defeated"? Oh, yes – the humiliation of it all!

At the time I had mixed feelings about the experience. I wish I had invested more time into knowing what being in a panto meant; it's relentless. I didn't have control of my days, something I have maintained for 35 years since leaving the army. I knew I had been given the job because I was Dame Kelly Holmes and not because of my theatre skills so at the end, when we took the bow, I was not initially addressing the audience because by tradition that's done by the lead, who was Brendan, and for me that was a real issue that I needed to sort.

Since realising the importance of owning my newfound voice, after my documentary was released in June 2022, I was suddenly feeling held back by the director and suppressed again in this difficult situation. I was so far removed from who I was that I decided I had to pipe up and stop myself from feeling pushed back again. So, I made a polite ask to Chris, the stage manager, and we decided that both Brendan and I would do the ending together – compromise is positive for everyone!

At the beginning of the run, I dreaded spending all that time with all the different cast members and I thought it would be suffocating. I realise now, looking back on it, I was only worried because I don't live in that world. Actors, singers, dancers, per-formers are all trying to be seen and heard and basically willing to put up with the intensity, the drama, the dictating, in pursuit of their next role or their lucky break – it's hard for them, but it's a must. I really enjoyed getting to know the younger cast members, it reminded me of being a young athlete, putting in the hard work for the results. You go through the highs and lows of your career and if you keep going you might just 'make it'.

The genuine positives are that I gained a lot of new knowledge from the whole process and got to know people who are very different to me and the industries I have worked in. While I sometimes struggled with the monotony of the role (doing the same things day in, day out) because I am used to doing four or five different events or interactions in my day, it was also quite therapeutic.

Having structure and being settled was strange for me after all these years, but it was also a relief to not have to think about everything and just follow a routine. Every morning I would get up, go for a run along the Hoe or go to the gym, have breakfast, do show one, lunch, evening show, pub. On one rare day off I took some of the cast to Devonport Naval Heritage Centre where we went on a decommissioned Submarine HMS Courageous, a veteran of the cold war. It's great still having my military connections and I know they all enjoyed it too.

Some of my friends and family made the trek down to Plymouth to watch and were delighted by my performances. Lou and I joined the cast most nights for drinks at the local bars or had lunch at the Barbican. We spent New Year's Eve out partying with the cast. Lou's Mum Mary and Aunt Anne came over from Belfast specially to watch me but also to ring it in, only to be the ones still wanting to party at 3am!

Our final performance was indescribable. By now I was saying whatever I wanted at the end of the show along with Brendan. I had gone past caring what I looked like, or whether I had fluffed the odd word, and had become proficient at masking any mistakes or blunders. My personality had also begun to shine through over the weeks in the many performances I did as I learned to just go with the flow. My first panto season was done!

All in all, I enjoyed being settled, doing something outside of my comfort zone, glad that I opened my mouth and forever grateful for the experience. I have always lived with the principle that 'if only' is too late and in this situation, I knew if I didn't try it, how would I know?

After panto everything changed. My entire outlook on myself and my life was transformed. I have been going to events, awards and shows for years, I am a global inspirational speaker, and it's only now that I am feeling 'present'. I'm no longer distracted by ruminations of the past or worries about the future but centred in the here and now. It's a great place to be. Let's put it another way. As I write this, I know my eyes are wide open.

I am looking at every opportunity to amplify the 'new' Kelly. Since this intense, almost spiritual realisation has hit me, I do not care what people think of me anymore. I feel in control of who I am and I'm on a mission to be unapologetically me.

I have been manifesting positivity for a few weeks now and it's been paying off. I have accepted being a perimenopausal woman and I am currently in control of the body pains by taking collagen – which has worked great for me. I've also begun combating my insomnia by darkening my room, regulating the temperature and basically not stressing about the time I fall asleep or when I wake up at night. To put it simply, it's less stressful not being stressed. My mental health is in a really good place at the moment. I am exercising regularly, setting myself goals. Homelife is good with Lou and Shiloh finally settled in after the big move.

A brief trip and rest in South Africa, 'my second home', inspired me to take a spontaneous and huge next step in my life. The sunrise in Africa is something else and after a trek to the top of the Lionhead at 6am, let's just say, she said yes!

On my return to the UK, I had an epiphany that I wanted to embrace the narrative around empowering women and organised my first Athena Effect event a week after International Women's Day as a result. The event was held and hosted by me in the ballroom at the Corinthia Hotel London and welcomed 175 women of all races, abilities, cultures, ages, sexual orientation, colour and status joined me. To have my vision come alive was incredible.

As Greek mythology goes, Athena the Olympian goddess of wisdom and war and the adored patroness of the city of Athens, was confident, practical, clever, a master of disguises and a great warrior. The energy, vibrancy, knowledge, wisdom, love and acceptance in the room that morning was mind blowing. It reminded me why I have achieved what drives me to still excel. I love supporting other people and bringing out the best in them, but I am also driven to keep achieving and re-inventing myself too.

I want women to support each other more and realise not only their power but their worth. Not because we are better than men, but because we should be equal. I am passionate about normalising conversation around diversity and inclusion for marginalised groups, pushing for equality so that people can live their lives with happiness and without judgement.

On April 19th this year, I reached the ripe old age of 39 + 15! Bloody hell, that's depressing. Sometimes I can't believe I still get such a rush of euphoria at this stage of my life, but then again, why not?

You've heard all my trials and tribulations in this book, now it's about my transformation – what's next? With some Olympic spirit and a positive mindset, I want to leave you with this; dreams can come true if you create them. To succeed is to believe in yourself, remember you are valid and worthy and don't let anyone dampen your fire. Mine still burns bright... Watch this space!

Acknowledgements

MY FIRST THANKS GOES TO EVERYONE WHO HAS bought this book and those who have followed me for years. You may not know me personally but have watched me grow, go through the highs and lows of my athletics career and life. I may never get to meet you or to say thanks personally, but I truly respect your dedication, your love and support, whoever you are.

To my Dad Mick. Your love has been unconditional since you took me into your life. I Love you x

To my bestie Kerrie and Miracle Woman Sandy (Kerrie's mum). Your love is undeniable, you will always be classed as my family. I love you from the bottom of my heart, always and forever.

To Debbie, (P.E. Teacher) and Dave Arnold (first coach in the sky), I hope your spirit can see me now. Without your guidance and belief in me as a little girl, I may never have had the courage to be who you knew I could be.

To my ever-growing family. Siblings; Lisa, Kevin, Stuart, Danny, Penny. Nieces and nephews; Honey, Archie, Lola, Rosa, Olivia, Lily, (future Lioness) Finley, Martha (Marmite) Poppy and Ada-Mae (another Lioness); Siblings in-law; Clare, Emma,

Dion and Danny's partner Kelly. No matter how we started or what we have done together, my love for you will be there until my dying day. Stay proud, work hard and never stop believing x

To Lara, Kim, Sarah, Sandra, Jackie, Dobo (who's in the sky), Wes, Flo, Emma, hairdressers Pat, Barbara, Trevor and Luci, make-up Emilie and Pilates Sandrine. You have been a huge part of my life at different times – thank you x

To my WRAC friends, you pushed me, and laughed with me. Whether I loved you or not, you are a big part of my early adult life. To Clare, Cathy, and other military comrades I have worked with in the past and recently, thanks for your acceptance and opportunities, they definitely added to my stories!

To Tess, Simon, Jo, Sheila and wider family, thanks for being part of my childhood, there were some great times.

To my 'inner circle' Kathy (side-kick), Polly, Kate, Suzanne-BG, Tracy. Beauty girls – Maria, Nicola, Belli, you all make me smile and I love our fun times together. Thank you for helping me trust people.

To Andrea my 'real' PA, well done and thanks for putting up for me for over ten years. You have had the hardest job of all sticking with me through my recent life transitions. Thanks again for all your support.

To everyone who has worked for and still works for my charity The Dame Kelly Holmes Trust, the impact we have made to transform the lives of young people has been extraordinary, thank you and keep up the great work.

To those who I have worked with or even had a romantic con-nection with in the past; however short or long. I believe people come into our lives to support, connect, fulfil, or challenge what we really want. I hope yours is now fruitful, safe and happy.

To ALL my 'Troopers' from my fitness community, Military

in Motion. I can't write all your names as I don't want to miss anyone out, but YOU know who you are; you saved me!

My new friends and acquaintances from the LGBTQIA community, allies and of course *Loose Women* and all the team that make it happen, thanks for helping me navigate this part of my life, it's been a life changing journey. I've had an blast and love getting to know you all.

Thank you to all the organisations for awards and accolades, in recognition of my dedication to the British Army, sport, community and charity over the years. I am truly grateful. A special shoutout to Polly and the team at The Pickering Cancer Drop-in Centre – I love you x

To all at Mirror Books, Reach Plc, ITV and Goalhanger for allowing me to share my deepest life struggles and successes, giving me a safe place and the freedom I always wanted, in this book and in my 2022 documentary *Kelly Holmes: Being Me.*

Finally – Remember that to have life, is to live life, we all deserve that!

Kelly, 2024